Poetic AMUSEMENT

Poetic AMUSEMENT

Raymond P. Hammond

ATHANATA ARTS, LTD.
Garden City, New York

ATHANATA ARTS, LTD.

Post Office Box 321

Garden City, New York 11530-0321

www.athanata.com

Printed in the United States of America

First Edition

Essays related to this work previously appeared in both *The New York Quarterly* and *The Quirk*.

Set in Myriad Pro

Layout and Design by Dylan R. Greif
Cover Photo by Inna Kleyman

ISBN-10: 0-9727993-3-8
ISBN-13: 978-0-9727993-3-1

The secret of poetry is silence…

– Charles Wright, *Quarter Notes*

TABLE OF CONTENTS

Poetry appears to be flourishing now more than ever with the abundance of poetry slams, contests, government funding, literary magazines, and a seemingly large audience. Many critics, however, decry that this is simply unsubstantiated shadow; that poetry is in fact in the throes of death. It is this paradox that is the topic of this book.

This book is not intended to belong to any particular school of thought, and in writing it, I did not ascribe to any manifesto or other organizational demand in forming my opinions. However, a nod should be given to the movement labeled "Expansive Poetry" since much of the current criticism regarding the creative writing workshop and Master of Fine Arts (MFA) programs originates in this camp. Many of the questions and arguments of the Expansive Poets parallel my own; however, I think that to ascribe to a particular group is severely limiting and taints one's thoughts with the same democratizing mediocrity that infects the workshop and inhibits independent thought. Movements themselves can be started by simply compiling an anthology, having a starting date, obtaining detractors, and, but not a necessity, writing a manifesto (Karr 49). Movements, though, come and go with the wind. It is the ideas which the movement is able to advance within literature that count.

Expansive poetry is a biform organism first labeled "Expansive" by Wade Newman in his 1988 essay: "Crossing the Boundary: The Expansive Movement in American Poetry." Elements of the Expansive Movement were previously designated as the New Formalism and the New Narrative movements. They both still retain their individuality and are often still referred to in these individual terms (Walzer 3).

Seen by some as a reaction to Postmodernism, Expansive poetry, Walzer contends, is considered Postmodern in nature, with complaint (22). Walzer gives two arguments in which Expansive poetry is critical: "First, and most obvious, Expansive poets believe that traditions are living, not dead" (22). Second, Walzer sees the Expansive poets as more sincere in their commitment to the mass culture than the traditional Postmodernists, whose "scholarship is seldom addressed at those who actually live in such [mass] culture" (23):

> Expansive poetry emerged in direct reaction against the entire academic culture that has been poetry's sole patron for a half a century. Expansive poetry aims to reach a general audience, using the materials of mass culture.[…] And it seems logical that accessible, but still good, poetry has a greater chance of doing so than Language poetry, which actively rejects accessibility. (Walzer 23–24)

Language poetry is the "other" movement rising out of the 1970s and 1980s concurrent with Expansive poetry (Walzer x). Expansive poetry encourages the use of form and narrative in poetry while Language poets:

> See language as the source of perception, and write difficult poems that reject lucidity in favor of exploring the varieties of meaning that language creates; their poems are heavily influenced by the mainstream of Postmodern theory, and have been quickly embraced by a theory-driven academy. (Walzer x)

Because of its proximity to the academy, Language poetry has not come into question as intensely as the Expansive poetry movement. Yet like Expansive poetry, Language poetry remains a fresh alternative to the workshop-type poems commonly produced in academia.

Walzer lists the "demands" of the Expansive poetry movement as they appeared in the essay, "Navigating the Flood," by Mark Jarman and Robert McDowell in the magazine *The Reaper*:

> 1. Take prosody off the hit list. 2. Stop calling formless writing poetry. 3. Accuracy, at all costs. 4. No emotion without narrative. 5. No more meditating on the meditation. 6. No more poems without poetry. 7. No more irresponsibility of expression. 8. Raze the House of Fashion. 9. Dismantle the Office of Translation. 10. Spring open the jail of the Self. (5)

This complaint of poetry is by no means new. But does this tendency of poems today necessarily spell an end to poetry as a whole? Throughout history, critics of poetry have written of the potential demise of poetry as an art form. Donald Hall states in *Death to the Death of Poetry* that he himself has "heard this lamentation for forty years [...]" (20). From allusions to the naysayers in Plato's "Ion" and Aristotle's "Poetics," to Longinus' addressing the questions of the aspiring poet Postumius Terentianus, to Dante's *De Vulgari Eloquentia*, to Percy Bysshe Shelley's answering Thomas Love Peacock in "A Defence of Poetry," to Edmund Wilson's "Is Verse a Dying Technique?," to Karl Shapiro's *The Poetry Wreck*, to Dana Gioia's *Can Poetry Matter?*, people have been trying to explain the loss of the poetic soul. As pointed out in *Death to the Death of Poetry*, Donald Hall states:

> Everything changes and everything stays the same. Poetry was always in good shape twenty or thirty years ago; *now* it has always gone to hell. I have heard this lamentation for forty years, not only from distinguished critics and essayists but from professors and journalists who enjoy viewing our culture with alarm. Repetition of a formula, under changed circumstances and with different particulars, does not make formulaic complaint invalid; but surely it suggests that the formula represents something besides what it repeatedly affirms. (20–21)

As Donald Hall concludes, the formulaic complaint is not invalid simply because it is cyclical. It must be examined for a more specific problem—flushing the substance of the problem from the shadows of the complaint. This cannot be done by simply ranting against what appears to be the problem—the poetry or the system—as most critics seem to be doing. The true essence must be developed of how these two elements are interacting to create a mediocre poetry. One of the inscriptions above the entrance to the Oracle of Delphi is τò τί, which can be simply translated as "What is it?" However, just the word τί asks that question. When it is coupled with the precedent τò the question becomes an imperative to seek exact precision in the answer. It is this principle that governed my investigation.

It is necessary to first examine the factors which set this time period apart from all those previous complaints in order to gain access to the specific essence of this cyclical complaint in contemporary American poetry. Dana Gioia, in his book, *Can Poetry Matter?*, addresses the first factor by observing the paradox that this complaint exists at a time when poetry seems to be flourishing. The fact of poetry's popularity, however, might well explain the following complaint:

> What is so special about our current scene—so discouraging—is the terrible vastness of the mass, volume, and weight of mediocrity that afflicts us. It is no longer a matter merely of closing the books with relief, the books we did not write, and leaving the dusty library behind. The dust accompanies us. At readings it fills our ears. It fills our mouths. And so we write, when we write, in a hurry, to be published quickly and with little attention paid to that which passes almost instantaneously into obscurity. The little that is to be learned, the little that is to be gained, being a poet in America today, or a reader of poetry, as measured against the degree of our longing and the indifference that is met, produces a factor in futility.
> (Kuzma 354)

Although mediocre verse has existed in all times, it is apparent that it has not appeared to be such a high percentage of the overall poetry being written as it does of that being written today. It is pervasive, and this is partly due to the second half of Greg Kuzma's statement: The pressure to publish exists more today than ever before. And not only is the pressure greater during this time, but that pressure stems from a unique source. This pressure to produce poetry is prevalent from the time the poets become students to the time they die; beginning with having to produce every week for a workshop, the poet then must produce in order to graduate from college, who then must produce in order to get a job, where they must produce in order to keep that job. In fact, most contemporary poets, as well as society itself, commonly identify those poets who are published as being "real poets," implying that those who are not published are somehow of a lesser class.

But the uniqueness of the current times is not limited to the poets themselves, as Vernon Shetley points out: "What is disturbing and novel about the situation of poetry today is that it has lost the attention not merely of common readers but of intellectuals, even many intellectuals whose chief interests are literary" (3). This leads us to another unique element of today: Those that do read poetry tend to think that they should be writing it:

> We have never before faced what it's like in the culture when hundreds of people want to write poetry and want to be instructed in it.[...] Now we are trying to instruct hundreds of beginning poets in the universities. We don't know how to instruct in that area. (Bly 318)

The ultimate differentiating factor that sets contemporary American poetry apart from all other times and locations; however, is the creation of the creative writing program:

> Why such an outburst at this time? Probably because of the very "industrialization" of creative writing that Berry had complained about; for in the dozens of creative writing programs, which had sprung up in imitation of the Iowa Writer's Workshop as its graduates spread out like missionaries through American colleges and universities, as American creative writing reached an "industrial" scale, the pressure upon young writers to master or to imitate the period style of the moment grew correspondingly more acute. It grew in direct proportion to the number of competing writers and the degree of the institutionalization of poetry. To attack the dominant mode of the moment was tantamount to attacking an institution. (Holden, *Fate* 24)

Poetic Amusement is a work of metacriticism. I decided to use this approach in lieu of preparing a typically Postmodern critical work incorporating one chapter of metacriticism, followed by a half dozen or so chapters of criticism of individual poets (usually collected loosely around the metacritical theme). A metacritical approach is ironic because metacriticism itself, and all other "meta-'s," is typically considered to be a resurgence within Postmodernism, although the actual technique of metacriticism dates back to the time of the Greeks (Wilson 106). The irony that comes to light is that I am using a predominately Postmodern technique to criticize another predominately Postmodern undercurrent—the neglect of historicity:

> Jameson notes that a major component of Postmodern-
> ism is "a weakening of historicity, both in our relationship
> to public History and in the new forms of our private tem-
> porality"—the loss of a sense of historical continuity and
> unity, replaced with a sense of a constant present. (Walzer
> 15)

To add to this irony, I am writing this book from an approach that reviews the entire history of criticism from the
earliest Greeks to the present critics.

I separate out the term metacriticism from the broader
category of Literary Theory because I do not intend this work
to establish or debate current trends in actual literary theory
or philosophy. Rather, this work is intended to utilize a historical approach to the criticism and theory to examine the
current societal impacts being imposed upon contemporary
American poetry. Moreover, this study examines that criticism of the cyclical complaint, as described above, for both
causes and cures of how poetry survived and how those principles can be applied to the unique problems of contemporary American poetry.

A "criticism of criticism" was chosen over the specific criticism of poets and poetry for numerous reasons. First, limiting
the discussion to specific literary examples would ultimately
limit the understanding of much broader principles applied
to various poems in slightly different ways. That is, if I were to
hold up a specific work as being the quintessential bad poem
or the ultimate good poem, I could create a misunderstand-
ing of the broader principle at hand. Secondly, the thought
of selecting one poet, school, or publisher as being the ex-

ample of what is wrong with contemporary American poetry would be misleading and wrong. This is not to say that there aren't poets, schools, and publishers in existence today that don't deserve to be named as the major contributors to the decline of contemporary American poetry, simply that it is not prudent to focus on unqualified rantings surrounding such specifics when the problem is much more pervasive and general. Lastly, history teaches us that the majority of mediocre verse will fall by the wayside as the literary canon fires back through time. The discussion in this book does not address the specifics of bad American verse, but rather the study of what is causing an increased mediocrity in the works that are beginning to survive those salvos of historicity.

For the purposes of this book, contemporary American poetry is defined as poetry written in the United States of America after 1967. This date coincides with the charter of the Associated Writing Programs, which, for the first time, organized all of the writing programs in this country into one representative organization. This date also casually applies to the generally accepted beginnings of Postmodernism in the 1960s (Walzer 11). This date also allows for the passing of one generation between the last major movement of influence, the Beats, and present; thereby allowing for the current generation of writers to be almost exclusively reared under the influence of an institutionally based poetics (Beach 7).

In attempting to describe the essence of poetry, I find it necessary, at times, to use the term "soul." Defining something as intangible as the "soul" could easily usurp the entire emphasis of the book. Although the essence that I am trying to explain is itself elusive and enigmatic, I approach the term from a circumambient perspective by utilizing the literary foundations established by tradition in an effort to ground the book in the scientific rather than the pseudo-scientific. Therefore, the term soul is both the life essence and the "principle of thought and action in man, commonly regarded as an entity distinct from the body [...]" ("Soul"). Therefore, I am using the term soul as life essence which exists as a result of that thought and action by a person, not as a spiritual being existing entirely independent of the physical body.

This book, above all else, is for me, a beginning. The researching and writing of each chapter have raised more and more questions regarding these topics, questions that I hope to eventually answer with further study. Each chapter could easily have filled a book in length, and for that reason each individual topic suffers slightly for the whole. In order to adequately answer the question at hand, each of these topics had to be addressed; therefore, they exist in order to answer that question and not as a complete investigation of each individual topic.

Poetic AMUSEMENT

CHAPTER ONE *poetic amusement*

A religious devotion to the truth, to the splendor of the
authentic, involves the writer in a process rewarding in
itself; but when that devotion brings us to undreamed
abysses and we find ourselves sailing slowly over them
and landing on the other side—that's ecstasy.

—Denise Levertov, *New and Selected Essays*

Amusement has become the most important, if not the sin-
gular preoccupation of American society. From sports and
sitcoms to Walt Disney, the fascination with amusement is
all consuming. Consider television shows dedicated to poetry; massive poetry conferences and festivals attended by
thousands; and spoken word shows travelling a performance
circuit like rock bands. Contemporary American poetry has
become deeply enmeshed in the midst of this great social
morass of amusement.

According to Donald Hall in *Death to the Death of Poetry*:
"More people write poetry in this country—publish it, hear
it, and presumably read it—than ever before" (22). Conse-
quently poems are being churned out at a greater rate today
than at any given time in history. More magazines are devot-
ed solely to poetry in this country than ever before and more
people are enrolled in Master of Fine Arts (MFA) programs
working on graduate degrees in poetry. However, as Dana
Gioia points out in *Can Poetry Matter?*: "The situation has
become a paradox, a Zen riddle of cultural sociology. Over

the past half century, as American poetry's specialist audience has steadily expanded, its general readership has declined" (2). The greater the number of poets that emerge, the smaller the specialty audience for each. In other words, most poets are read only by other poets and, in some cases, read only by that poet's friends and family. One organizer in New York lamented the necessity of canceling an event because the poet's friends and family could not attend. The relatively well-known poet chose to cancel the reading rather than risk an unappreciative audience.[1]

The paradoxical resurgence of poetry seems as gilded and as superficial as the media by which it is touted. This fact rings true especially when the quality of most contemporary poetry is taken into consideration—a quality that is seemingly in decline. Karl Shapiro writes in *The Poetry Wreck*:

> We are experiencing a literary breakdown which is unlike anything I know of in the history of letters. It is something new and something to be reckoned with. We have reached the level of mindlessness at which students and the literate public can no longer distinguish between poetry and gibberish. (362)

This statement was written in February 1970, and, though much has happened regarding the state of American poetry since then, the gist of what Shapiro claimed is truer today than ever before. Reading thousands of submissions each year for *The New York Quarterly*, the editorial staff finds that few, if any, poems hold the interest of the readers from beginning

---

1   Personal observation.

to end, much less strike them dumbfounded or even cause them to pause and reflect.[2] Most are predictable drivel—the incest poem, the taxi ride poem, the homeless person poem, the "I hate/love my father poem," the "my boyfriend dumped me and now I am pissed poem." Most contemporary poets attempt to end their poems with the proverbial epiphany, built around one interesting line or thought. Often, it is this line which is the only salvageable part of the whole poem. It is this line or thought that is generally noticed on the first reading, and is good on its own merits, just not good enough to build an entire poem around. These poems, as J. D. Mc-Clatchy says, are

> the everyday life of psychopathology, the penny dreadfuls of domesticity, the software of sensibility, surrealism with a heart, Zen advertising copy, urban chanties, epiphanies around the backyard barbecue, work songs for the twice-divorced kitchen brigade, political solipsism, the folkways of the New Journalism, minimalism on a gigantic scale, the thumbed-smooth small coin of the realm (in denominations of Soul, Pain, Stone, Wind, and You). (*White Paper* 9)

These often cutesy observations or simple revelations only serve to make the ordinary mundane.

Some poets even explain the image either in the text of the poem or in Eliotesque footnotes. Still others provide notes or explain themselves in their cover letters just in case you fell off a wagon more remote than theirs. As Karl Shapiro says, "The poet therefore has no obligation to 'explain'

---

2 Personal experience.

his poem in other terms, for there is nothing to explain unless something has gone wrong" (*Poetry Wreck 260*). Telling rather than showing, these poems miss most poetic devices including meter and rhyme even in their most subtle, free verse forms. In enumerating what exactly is wrong with contemporary American poetry, Mary Kinzie observes:

> Indeed, it would appear that even in much fervent and accomplished descriptive, meditative, and conversational verse today, mental and imaginative constructs are hobbled by a limited knowledge of and attention to discursive and rhetorical devices (figures of speech) and tropes (figures of thought), not to mention a flattened prosody. This latter limitation is compounded by the fact that the lineation, typography, and use of whitespace to control rhythm and attention too often come down, at best, to a mildly appealing visual and cognitive pattern or, at worst, to a secret (not shared) compositional aid. (303)

It is exactly the lack of tropes and rhetorical devices, coupled with the flatness of language that leads one to think that most contemporary American poetry is simply poorly written prose arbitrarily divided into line breaks.[3] J. D. McClatchy agrees that there is a flatness of language: "Not only is the language of most contemporary poems—as distinct from their animating emotions—not heightened, but its very flatness is a symptom of unplanned obsolescence" (*White Paper 10*). According to Mary Karr, absence of emotion and lack of clarity are the two sins popular in today's poetry (52). While

---

3   See Chapter 3 for a full discussion on this topic.

Donald Hall sees workshop poems as:

> Often readable, charming, funny, touching, sometimes even intelligent. But they are usually brief, they resemble each other, they are anecdotal, they do not extend themselves, they make no great claims, they connect small things to other small things. […] I do not complain that we find ourselves incapable of such achievement; I complain that we seem not even to entertain the desire. ("Ambition" 230)

In a feature article in *The New York Quarterly*, "The Present State of American Poetry," guest author Todd Moore wrote:

> Bukowski would say, there is no gamble and he'd be absolutely dead center right. There is no gamble, no risk, no heart, no cock, no cunt, no crotch, no asshole, no blood, no human organs of any kind. But plenty of stink. Mainstream American poetry stinks all to hell. It's a rotting corpse that the crows and the buzzards won't even touch. Maybe it is written by real living breathing humans, but they leave scarcely a trace of humanity in their work. Their words lie dead on the page and I can't help but wonder if any of the so called major American poets would write a poem that they'd die for. Would scratch something out on the back of an old envelope they knew they'd be stood up against the wall for. I can't remember the last time I read a poem that even figuratively speaking gave me a mild headache let alone took the top of my head off. (109)

The answer, of course, to Todd Moore's inherent question is that most contemporary poets have not taken risks, have not had to back their bodies up against a wall to protect their poems, have not taken a beating for what they believe. Poets today take no risk in their lives or their poetry. In speaking about what he calls the "legitimation crisis," Walter Kalaidjian states:

> This tension continues to be most deeply felt by academics, whose everyday professional lives deny the consoling models of community that humanism traditionally espouses. For better or for worse, most of our enduring verse writers are academics whose poetry typically seeks to repress and transcend their institutional lives. Often reproducing the professional regimen and bureaucratic functioning of the corporate world, academe has a hand in defining the writer's role, mixing its discourse little by little with poetry's lyric rhetoric. (26–27)

Longinus wrote in the third century A.D. that: "Inferior and average talent remains for the most part safe and faultless because it avoids risk and does not aim at the heights [...]" (45). Donald Hall sees this lack of risk as a lack of ambition: "But if failure is constant, the types of failure vary, and the qualities and habits of our society specify the manners and the methods of our failure. I think that we fail in part because we lack serious ambition" ("Ambition" 229).

It is without this ambition, this striving, this seeking of the self that the in-authenticity of contemporary American poetry becomes apparent. A "something else," which should resonate within us as we read a poem, as it did for Emily Dickinson when she wrote that it should feel like the top of her head had been taken off, is noticeably absent. No inward screams of existence develop for the small coterie of contemporary readers of poetry—such as existed in Walt Whitman's barbaric yawp—only the outward stench of mediocrity.

Several years ago a travelling poetry show landed in a New Orleans bar that catered to a regular crowd of music fans. Between the featured band's sets, Spoken Word poets would get up and read their boring palaver, trying to shock the crowd with tales from the local insane asylum and a continual assault of the audience with the word "fuck." During this show, a few of the local die-hard poets were up front and attentive during these sessions, but most of the music fans ignored the poets. At the last of these breaks, one of the organizers got up and chastised the rest of the audience for milling around and for their indifference to the poets. The speaker even made an obscene gesture toward the audience at the end of his speech about "poets bringing the truth." A riot should have ensued. But no one cared enough to get upset either for or against the poems being read, much less start a good old fashion barroom brawl. The band resumed its performance and the incident was soon, sadly, forgotten by all.[4]

These screams simply do not exist. If the poets are not putting these primal screams into the poems, then there is no way that an audience can be expected to resonate with the poem. Furthermore, in today's society the general reader accepts these flat poems because they themselves have been numbed by the mass amusement which surrounds them on a daily basis:

---

4 Personal experience.

> Poetry of the greatest cultural importance has historically dealt with those aspects of reality in which people found their identity and security. But society in which many people find their chief security and sense of meaning through commercial products, from the possession of certain objects, will produce great advertising, not great poetry; the things most available for use as symbols are not of enough long-term importance to support serious art. (Clausen 120–121)

In the age of television and the internet, minds are turned off, and thinking is done in flashing bursts of thought that resemble the loud and strobing shallow images that are blasted across television and movie screens.

As Bukowski reminds us: "Whitman said, 'To have great poetry we must have great audiences.' No, we must have great poetry, then perhaps we will have great audiences. Nobody reads the stuff now because there's no juice, fire, adventure, dance and truth to it" (280).

Another group, though, falls between the poet and the reader in sharing responsibility for the downward spiral of contemporary American poetry—the critics. Randall Jarrell reminds us that "the first demand that is made upon any real critic: He must stick his neck out just as the artist does, if he is to be of any real use to art" (87). But, just as contemporary poets, contemporary critics also are caught in the poetry industry's web and fail to take risks: "When not only one's reputation but one's salary is at stake, the ante is upped exponentially [...]. It is thought bad form to review one's peers other than applausivley. [...] [T]hey will only review books they are certain they can praise" (Disch 4). Edwin Muir states that criticism is to be "a helpful intermediary between literature and the reader—and it has a duty to both" (61). According to Horace, this duty is to be, above all else, an honest critique (Horace 445–447). If criticism fails in this regard and only provides a positive criticism of the work, then it misses the even larger value of honesty because it calls into suspicion the flattery it propounds: "The larger value of negative criticism—beyond the sigh of relief that 'At last someone has said it'—is that without it, any expression of delight or enthusiasm is under suspicion of being one more big hug in that special-education classroom where poets minister to each other's needs for self-esteem" (Disch 228). As Joyce Henning once told Douglas Treem: "One should only criticize that which one loves or that which one feels is evil" (qtd. in "Interview").

American democracy has ensured that every person can become an accredited poet if he or she spends the time and money to endure an MFA program in writing or enroll in a few workshops. Since many of these programs are low residency and require only a couple of weeks a year on campus, many MFA programs can now be completed without the poet moving to the campus or even leaving home for any time period longer than that of a standard vacation. Often seen as a license, an MFA degree ensures the poet a place within the "good old boy network."

This attitude extends far beyond the academy. The sheer mass of poetry produced and submitted in this country is staggering. Poets often submit "occasion poems" before the event they are writing about has even left the front page of the newspaper. Take, for instance, the death of Princess Diana. *The New York Quarterly* received numerous submissions written about this tragedy all postmarked within a week of her death. The managerial systems the poets utilize to track their poems is equally impressive and often quite complex with the use of coded envelopes and manuscripts. Many of the submissions received by *The New York Quarterly* are accompanied by form letters, often stuffed so hurriedly into the envelope that the salutation on the letter and the address on the envelope do not match. Some contemporary poets use literary agents to generate their submissions. Others use a "shotgun" method of submitting to every magazine listed in the *Poet's Market*, whether or not their poems are appropriate. Many have never even seen *The New York Quarterly* prior to submission and freely admit this in their cover letters. Still others include cover letters containing everything from full page lists of publication credits, to self-promotional flyers, to pleas of poverty or ignorance, to death threats if their poems are not published. This publication feeding frenzy is spawned by the poetry industry which has become insatiable for mediocrity. With numerous new poetry magazines hitting the market every year, the need to publish has become immediately gratifiable. As Donald Hall said: "Poems have become as instant as coffee or onion soup mix" ("Ambition" 237).

Horace admonishes us against this practice and demonstrates the sheer stupidity of this publication frenzy through the simplicity of this thought:

> *You* will compose and complete nothing against the grain (you have too much sense and taste). If you do write something later, be sure to read it aloud to the critic Tarpa, and also to your father and me. Then hold it back 'till the ninth year,' keeping your jotter inside the house. You can always

delete what hasn't been published; a word let loose is gone forever. (385–390)

Contemporary poets could not imagine keeping their poems for almost ten years before "letting them loose." After all, "Quality is all very well, but it is *not* democratic […]. Democracy demands the interchangeable part and the worker on the production line […]" (Hall, "Ambition" 234–235). It is this interchangeability of the poems, the poets and the voices that is at the heart of the mediocrity in contemporary American poetry:

> For me it is impossible to distinguish between one of these marvelous mechanical poems and another. They always seem to me to be written by the same person or Thing. I can't name five poets writing in the English or American language today who have enough individuality or style to be distinguished from one another. That some get ahead of others in reputation is purely a matter of chance. Or so I believe. (Shapiro, *Poetry Wreck* 238)

The poetry industry exists for one reason and one reason alone: the poetry industry. The publishers wish to publish, the gamesters wish to game, the readers wish to read, the teachers wish to teach, and the poets wish to publish as quickly and as much as possible; and none of it has anything to do with poetry. The poetry industry has fallen into the same trap of consumerism as the rest of our culture, a commercial verse market, so called by Walter Kalaidjian (35).

Poetry is inauthentic because it is cranked out at a phenomenal rate. This inauthenticity heralds the same gilding as the rest of the consumeristic society. Poetry has become mass produced for the masses for amusement. But why are the poems considered flat, drab, and lacking souls just because they are mass produced? If we consider the term "amusement" in an extremely literal sense, the true essence of the problem is exposed: Contemporary poetry exists without a Muse.

CHAPTER TWO ***the poetry industry***

One's-Self I sing, a simple separate person,
Yet utter the word Democratic, the word En-Masse.

—Walt Whitman, *Leaves of Grass*

The Muse has been replaced in contemporary America by a poetry industry that both caters to, and is created by, the masses. The poetry industry, which is dependent upon the seedbeds of both public assistance and academia for its sustenance, is solidly democratic in nature:

> As colleges and universities expanded to keep pace with demographic trends, higher education in America became democratized as it never had been before. The sixties saw democratization of poetry (and of high culture in general), the scale of which is accurately measured by Berry's word "industry." Virtually all the main trends in poetry during the late sixties and early seventies–stylistic as well as institutional–can be in part or else entirely attributable to "democratization." (Holden, *Fate* 20)

A democracy's ability to thrive depends upon a large middle class. It also depends upon the rule of the majority. Both of these factors create a dependence upon the median.

From strip malls to Mickey Mouse, our society is one in which a middle class and resultant ambivalence toward the arts flourishes. Most poetry written today reflects this mediocrity:

> When an art form is produced en masse, most of it will conform to the fashion of the moment, be merely competent. But why feign surprise or disappointment at this? Mediocrity is present in every human endeavor. Indeed, it is prevalent *by definition*, it is a statistical fact: In every statistical sample, there is a "median," "the value, equaled or exceeded by exactly half of the values in a given list."
> (Holden, *Fate* 14)

The problem comes not from the presence of mediocrity; it will be, and has always been, present. The problem stems from the mass over production of mediocre quality poems and the institution of certain facets particular to our society that not only maintain but also serve to advance the mediocre. As suggested by Gresham's Law, enough mediocre poetry will eventually drive out the good. At this point, the democratization of poetry becomes a bad influence (Hollander 169).

The absence of passion in contemporary American poetry stems, in part, from a basic absence of investment. This fact is not surprising given that one of the greatest instruments of the democracy is the use of the committee in lieu of personal decision making. From government to corporate offices, to the small town church, this averaging device has become prevalent within our society. The world of poetry has also been infected by this committee mindset, manifested in the poetry workshop.

Beginning in 1895 with the first course in creative writing offered at the University of Iowa, the workshop was a reaction to the mystique of writing which had been heralded by the Romantics and taken to the point of absurd by the Modernists:

> Not unexpectedly, critical idolatry of Art, the artist, and the aesthetic soon brought about a demystifying reaction, something along the lines of stock market correction for geniuses. In tandem with this spirit, oddly enough, the creative writing workshop was born. (Grimes 19)

Reminiscent of the French Academy in the 1700s, and echoing almost exactly the same results, the writing workshop would live to see a similar Waterloo of mediocrity:

> The [French Academy] performed a great service in breaking the stranglehold of the guilds on the training of artists, in raising the standards of art instruction, and in improving the status of artists. On the other hand, it locked the artist into a closed system, made conformity a virtue, and treated individualism and originality of style as sins to be avoided at all costs. By standardizing methods of instruction, it also standardized the bases of critical judgement. [...] Academicism established above all the principle that the artist succeeded not through native genius but through a correctness of technique that could only be acquired through proper training. ("Practice and Profession of the Arts...")

This paragraph could easily have been written about the creative writing workshop and MFA programs of today. Karl Shapiro states in his 1970 article: "I have been engaged in creative writing programs for twenty-odd years, virtually from the beginning of this kind of teaching. These programs have corroded steadily and today have reached the point of futility" (355).

Consistent with the democratic society in which we live, poetry committees are convened of persons seeking validation and a community for their own work. In the traditional workshop, the poet is not allowed to speak once the poem has been presented for criticism. A form of "impressionism" (Semansky 69) is then employed under the title of "close reading" by the other members of the workshop:

> What is judged in Workshop, generally by the process of "close reading," is the executed result of the author's intentions. Workshop doesn't care about what you meant to say, or how you feel about what you said; it cares about what was said, the "words on the page." Like New Criticism, it examines texts without regard to authorial desire. (Grimes 20)

In this respect, the workshop is a positive influence on the burgeoning young poet. Because the workshop provides a knowledgeable audience for his or her work, the young poet is able to see first hand how an audience will receive the work.

However, the mediocrity imposed by the "committee" atmosphere quickly outweighs any positive attributes:

At first blush the workshop classroom may appear more "democratic," less dogmatic than a lecture format whose locus is the teacher as repository of knowledge. However, the apparently democratized market of the workshop with its emphasis on the free exchange of ideas is itself constrained by the boundaries drawn up in the discourse on craft, a discourse that requires the student first to submit to class analysis before he or she can own the final version of his or her own poem. (Semansky 139)

Generally consisting of a random cross section of literary Americana, this committee will ultimately beat the individuality out of a poet through peer pressure and politics, replacing the poet's voice with its own middle-American mediocrity:

Committees are notably stupid; they vote for mediocrity, their mind is the least common denominator. Even if there are a few intelligent members, the unintelligent members will be the ones with spare time, and they will get about trying to 'run the committee,' trying to get in new members who will vote for their kind of inanity. *Et cetera, ad infinitum.* (Pound, *Essays* 223)

The responsibility of agonizing revisions and decisions are left to a committee's caucus rather than to the gut tendencies of an artist who is willing to sacrifice for his art. The resultant work is left gang raped and abandoned in a dumpster, barely recognizable. Once the individual voice has been tempered by the opinions of the masses, there is no way a poem can still possess an individual "soul." In the workshop format, just like in a corporate committee, compromises are made, recommendations are heard and accepted or rejected, and persuasions abound. This opens the door for politics to enter the poetic process as members of the workshop campaign for their own point of view. The resulting poem is often dependent upon the one in the group who has the strongest will or loudest bark rather than the individual voice of the poet.

By allowing graduate students to present a body of creative work in lieu of a critical thesis, the concept of the graduate creative writing program was born in 1931, again at Iowa (Semansky 11). The creative writing workshop would become the heart of the graduate creative writing curriculum. However, a World War, two significant military actions, the lingering presence of great writers such as Pound, Moore, Eliot, H. D., Williams, Millay, Auden, Thomas, Yeats, etc., and the rise of two poetic genres, the Beats and the Confessionals, all contributed to preventing the writing program concept from flourishing until the late 1960s. Now given their official sanction by most programs adopting the terminal degree of an MFA, by the late 1960s several dozen graduate creative writing programs would begin to emerge throughout the country. In 1967, the AWP was established to organize these creative writing programs. In 1976, a new element was added by Goddard College in Plainfield, Vermont, whereby one could obtain a graduate degree through a low-residency study. This low-residency allows students to study at home and only report to campus for ten days every six months. People would no longer have to commit even so much as two years of their lives to intensive study of poetry; they could now write poems in their spare time much like doing embroidery or building a ship in a bottle. Essentially an American phenomenon (Semansky 15), the creative writing program is also exclusively a contemporary phenomenon:

> The notion of a classroom education for creative writers (or those who used to be called simply poets) is less than three-quarters of a century old. When it first came into existence as a subject of instruction, creative writing was a novelty. Nothing quite like it had previously appeared. Writers had been educated before, and they had learned their lessons, but not in schools. This is not to say that prior to our time poets were unschooled; or that the question of how to educate a poet was never raised; or that poets did not need to learn their art. But when they went to school, the poets did not receive an education which was restricted and specifically oriented to their practice as poets. Their school work was not confined to the current practice of already established poets. No age prior to our own has established an institution remotely resembling the graduate writer's workshop. For most of literary history, indeed, a poet was formally educated like any other educated person. (Myers 18–19)

Indeed it is hard for one to imagine a workshop with Homer, or Dante, or Shakespeare in attendance or even to imagine they would have needed such a contrivance. Thomas M. Disch alludes to this when he says: "Talent of the larger sort doesn't need workshops, as the history of literature bears ample witness" (157).

The concept of the MFA in writing degree programs,

19

though, has snowballed. Between its inception in 1967 and Chris Semansky's dissertation, the AWP's membership grew from 13 programs to 328 in 1990. PhDs were available in 31 of these programs and 50 MFA programs and 140 MA programs existed (Semansky 2). In 1997 401 programs were registered with the AWP. Of those, 30 offered PhDs, 74 offered MFAs and 142 offered MAs or MSs (this author's count, *AWP Guide*). Although the dramatic rise in numbers of programs seems to be leveling off, it is clear that the general trend is still steadily on the increase.

As Christopher Beach points out: "Without question, the most significant demographic shift in American poetic culture over the past one quarter century has been the growth of the creative writing academy" (4). What, then, accounts for this irony? If one does not need to participate in one of these programs to become a great writer, as evidenced by history, why then has the number of programs risen over 300% since the inception of the AWP?

The answer lies in the fact that poets bedded down with the universities in an attempt to secure their financial futures. Once there, however, the deans came to realize that writing programs were an untapped resource of income for their colleges and universities, as noted by Eve Shelnutt: "A number of English Departments owe their fiscal security to writing programs" (8).

In contemporary American society most readers of poetry see the type of work being produced and think, "why not? Why can't I learn to be a poet?"

In this totalitarian democracy, people not only love poets, they want to *be* poets. They want to think critically, to act openly and to write significantly. Because poetry has been thoroughly democratized, there's a lot of poetry around. (Reeve 709)

The answer is that they can now be a poet, anyone can, complete with the credentials of an accredited university. The writing programs have accomplished exactly what they had set out to do—demystify writing:

He [the student] has but to make the formal application, and hand over the money. In class he will learn how much fun writing is, and how easy it is. He will learn how to write poems in sentences of no more than six words, how to use colors for their evocative power, how to get a simple word like "against" to provide nearly all the energy in an otherwise exhausted poem. (Kuzma 349)

With their validation and certification as a poet coming in only two years, anyone in America can launch themselves directly into "po' biz" with little or no effort. Once the student has gone through this accreditation, however, they soon begin to question what has happened to them:

Many MFA students come to realize that they are learning not so much how to write poetry as how to be academic poets: They are acquiring the socialization necessary to mold themselves as professional poets, as well as the networking skills and connections they will need to pursue a career in an increasingly tight academic market. (Beach 11)

And tight that market has become. With literally hundreds of newly dubbed "poets" entering the job market each year, teaching jobs are becoming harder and harder to find:

> The exponential growth of the university creative writing program, a growth that created tremendous professional opportunities for poets throughout the 1960s, 1970s, and 1980s, has now created a difficult situation for those poets not already securely employed within the system. Further, the rapidly growing poetry culture that has been nurtured by the creative writing environment has now far outstripped the university's capacity to accommodate it, and it is becoming increasingly difficult for new poetry MFAs to find regular teaching positions. (Beach 5)

As Charles Bukowski reminds us, most people forget that poetry can be written by "a bus driver, a field hand or a fry cook" (199). The jobs that do exist for graduating poets are becoming increasingly reliant upon "badges of honor" to make their selections. Simply scouring over random job listings sent out by the AWP, I discovered these badges of honor include the winning of poetry contests, an MFA degree, which is almost always a must, as well as the ever present "significant creative publication" requirement.

These requirements add up to the formation of an exclusive club that buoys the entire creative writing teaching profession in America: "The MFA remains a virtual requirement for most creative writing jobs, and without it the academy is a closed field for most poets" (Beach 13). And more incestuously:

Current practices in hiring writing faculty also tend to in-
sure that the "old boy" system of hiring former classmates
or friends of friends or cohorts from a dozen AWP conven-
tions will narrow the range of perspectives offered by a
writing program. (Shelnutt 14)

Because of the "publish or perish" mentality and the
need to be published in order to secure a job, an "iron curtain" extends into the publishing arena in the form of a "good
old boy" network: "Today the 'New Academy' of the creative
writing program has similarly raised a kind of iron curtain of
poetic writing, walling in a mainstream practice while excluding from its borders the work of an experimental, countercul-
tural, or avant-garde mode" (Beach 8). This type of exclusion
necessarily leads to a sameness within the ranks of the privi-
leged. As Christopher Beach states, "The university system
now functions as the major screening mechanism for the poetry culture, a means of including some poets and excluding
others; it also functions more subtly as a mechanism for making hierarchical distinctions concerning the most prestigious
programs and poets" (4).

This sameness infects the MFA students for several reasons. First, conformity is the name of the game if one wants
to excel within the poetry industry. Therefore, one learns to
write like other contemporary American poets in order to
win contests, because the contests are judged by those same
contemporary American poets. These students also conform
because they need to network in order to publish their work.
They conform in their writing because they need to complete their MFA in order to compete in the job market. Tied
in with completing the MFA is the need, on a weekly basis,

to produce a poem for review in the workshop. Producing poetry on such a regular basis and for such specific reasons, the poet begins to produce poetry in order to either impress the teacher or peers in the workshop, or to enhance his or her career. The university, then, becomes the legitimizing aspect for the poet's work (Beach 7).

However, the MFA programs are also vested in the student's publication credits. By touting both students and graduates who have published or won awards, the MFA programs make subliminal promises that if you attend their program, you will get published or win awards. In a recent issue of *The Writer's Chronicle* (September 1999) a full-page ad ran on the last page for Western Michigan University's Creative Writing Program. In a column prominently placed in the upper right hand half of the page was a list of three students who had recently published or won awards.

A lucrative business also exists of big name poets travelling from program to program as "visiting faculty." These names, no doubt, are to assist in the baiting of prospective students: "The primary goal of many programs, according to Shelnutt, is not to offer the best possible education, but to attract the largest possible number of students and to make sure those students have made the connections necessary to publish when they graduate" (Beach 13).

In order to keep the students they have, MFA programs will not only over encourage their students (Bly 257), but some will go so far as to make changes to please the student population in order to keep that economic base (Shelnutt 16). However, as Eve Shelnutt proclaims: "Writing programs do not need to produce more writers, contrary to all the trends in universities that tout 'bigger as better.' [...] Writing programs need to produce *better* writers for whom the latest fads in fiction and poetry are to be questioned" (23). This insatiable financial need by the MFA programs to constantly attract students leads to a sheer mass of people applying to and attending these programs. However, as Greg Kuzma points out: "The writer no longer teaches the few who really care and are dedicated to the art, the few and the best, he teaches the average and the many" (344).

The question, then, is whether the creative writing programs can accomplish this goal and actually teach poets to be poets. The answer to this question is a resounding "maybe." Think of learning to ride a bicycle. One can be taught all of the physics and mechanics surrounding the operation of the bicycle, and can have a great deal of practice riding the bicycle with training wheels. But until those training wheels have come off, and the bicycle wobbles to a straight path for the first time under the rider's own power and balance, the bicycle has not actually been ridden. The same is true about poetry. Craft can be taught, the summoning of the Muse can not: "And it is absolutely impossible to teach someone in any external fashion how to find these infinitely small moments: They are found only when a man gives himself to his feeling" (Tolstoy 100).

What can be taught, however, is the technical aspects of poetry. It is this craft of poetry on which the MFA and creative writing programs have come to focus. Because they think that the Muse can not be taught, they have demystified poetry thereby removing the elements they thought they could not teach (Grimes 19). This demystification, however, is seen by Semansky as "A key component in rationales for creative writing's place in the curriculum. But it exists almost exclusively at the level of student practice. Remystification, however, is equally important by clarifying distinctions between the amateur and the professional" (98). This remystification supposedly takes place, magically, upon graduation, but by neglecting the Muse altogether, the students are never prepared for this remystification process.

For the most part, creative writing and MFA programs teach a curriculum which primarily consists of the writing of poetry in preparation for the workshop, the critiquing of the fellow student's work in the workshop, and the reading of poetry: "Where the poetry that is studied is, by and large, the poetry that is written there—by fellow students, by their instructors, and by those with whom their instructors network, poets visiting to give a reading" (Disch 9). By limiting the students' intake of poetry to that of exclusively contemporary American, the academy has instilled an unmistakable sameness which Chris Semansky refers to as "the poetics of experience": "I refer to the loose, free verse lyrics and narratives, usually written 'about' some experience the writer has had. The tone is often conversational, the diction colloquial. The abundance of these kinds of poems in literary journals and in workshops themselves has become an almost universal staple of criticism about the programs […]" (86–87).

As Thomas M. Disch observes:

> [Workshop students have] no sense of the history embedded in their own tongue. Even in their own language they will have read only a smattering of its classics, and they will have been taught to dismiss most of that as fusty, patristic, and irrelevant […]. (8)

This is one of the major areas where creative writing programs could prepare the students for the eventual remystification of poetry. Creative writing programs need to acknowledge that: "Writers have to start out as readers, and before they put pen to paper, even the most disaffected of them will have internalized the norms and forms of the tradition from which they wish to secede" (Heaney 6). By providing a literary tradition to push up against these programs could instill the necessary stewardship for that tradition which helps to create the Muse, thereby remystifying the process.

Another major component of study neglected in the creative writing program is that of critical theory. As Eve Shelnutt points out:

> And students who may never upon graduation, write about writing are nonetheless at a disadvantage as creative writers if they lack sufficient training by which to evaluate the implications of new formal devices in writing that begin as fads. (10)

The development of a "critical eye" is to be closely discerned from "critiquing" which takes place in the workshop. Critiquing is simply a skill that requires the student to be a good sight reader, to borrow a musical term. By critiquing the other students' poems, the poet develops basic skills in assessing how closely a poem conforms to the norm set in front of the class as exemplary of how to write poetry. The development of a critical eye, however, allows the poet to place the poem within a historical context (Shelnutt 8) and examine it closely within the context of literary theory. Both of these systems are crucial if the poet is to advance his or her own poetic voice beyond that of the workshop "norm."

Most medical jobs require either certification or licensing prior to allowing patient contact. Many of these jobs—paramedic, registered nurse, licensed practical nurse, respiratory therapist—require many hours of familiarization with the equipment and tools that are to be used as a part of their training and certification. Since many view the MFA as not only a rite of passage, but as a certification to write poetry, why is it that there is no training in the use of the tools necessary to write poetry? It has already been shown that both stewardship and critical theory are missing from the poet's toolbox; the third missing tool is the English language.

Respiratory therapists do not arrive at respiratory therapy school knowing all there is to know about a respirator. Just as the respirator is the primary tool of the respiratory therapist, in America, the English language is the primary tool of the poet. It should not be presumed, then, that the MFA student already knows all there is to know about the English language. Aside from basic grammar skills, the poet should at least be familiarized with the history of the English language, which is generally a required course for most traditional English majors. This is especially important considering that Ezra Pound said "Good writers are those who keep the language efficient" (*ABC*, 32). The language, then, is both the poets' tool and commission; they need to know all they can about that tool to carry out the commission.

By neglecting to teach the basics the students require to develop as poets, and by subjecting them to both demystification and isolation, the resultant poetry is a "deadly sameness of verse" which John Hollander attributes to its having become academic (171). Donald Hall refers to these workshop products as "McPoems," ("Ambition" 235) and Joseph Epstein observes that poetry has been "taken out of the world, chilled in the classroom, and vastly overproduced by men and women who are licensed to write it by degree if not necessarily by talent or spirit" ("Who Killed Poetry?" 20). By virtue of this attention only to craft, demystification, and isolation, the true creative writer becomes lost:

> The unfortunate writer, who took up writing poems or stories, not as a "career choice" advised him by some guidance counselor or marketing extrapolator, but because he was compelled to do so, and can do nothing else, "creative writing" […], is a disaster. (Kuzma 344)

According to David Myers, however, creative writing did not start out by neglecting these components: "In the beginning, the purpose of creative writing was not to establish a profession for writers but to educate a new type of writer who was a blend of the critic and the creator" (196).

the socialization of poetry

The singer Tom Robinson once said that the state called success which society gives is really a bribe. For contemporary American poets, the delusion of academic success, grants, and publication becomes that bribe. Other factors exist within the community that are not necessarily based in academia, but still have the same democratizing effects and encourage

mediocrity. These include the funding of poets and magazines by governmental agencies, poetry contests, specialized
anthologies, and poetry readings.

The National Endowment for the Arts (NEA), which was
founded in 1965 under the Johnson administration, has had
a significant impact upon the way poetry is written, paid for,
and appreciated. This impact has upset the balance, allowing for the survival of a few poets chosen not on the quality
of their work, but on how well they play the system. This forc-
es many poets to compromise in order to compete. The selecting officials become the establishers of taste by deciding
which poets are allowed into the mission for soup and which
ones are turned out into the cold to fend for themselves.

Robert Bly views the NEA as "domesticating" the poet and
"an even worse catastrophe, in the long run, to the ecology
of poetry than the universities" (301). Thomas M. Disch views
the NEA as a "free lunch":

> My objection to a "free lunch" mentality—i.e., to the sense
> of entitlement that poets (and other Guggenheim, and
> NEA applicants) have come to share with the homeless
> and other self-styled victims of the System—is that it is
> debilitating, demoralizing, and self-deluding. Self-delud-
> ing for the simple reason that the world doesn't owe us a
> living. (68–69)

Poets use poetry contests (actual contests, not the ones
in the Sunday comics) as another stamp of validation and
worse yet another credit required for admittance into the
"club." Poets parade these contests around in their cover letters and résumés like so many badges of honor. Some con-

tests, like the Pushcart Prize, have become so highly favored among most poets that they list in their résumés each time they were nominated.[5] The poetry contest, however, serves only as another tool of standardization. The results are completely at the discretion and influence of each judge. One does not submit a poem after the style of Pound to a contest that is to be adjudicated by Maya Angelou. And, if one did they would certainly not expect to win. This limits the example of what is good to what suits the tastes of the judge, and more often than not, that taste is very similar to his or her own work. However, contests become the epitome of democracy when they are judged not by one voice, but by a committee of voices coming to agreement not on the best poem, but on the poem most median to everyone's liking.

Poets often use the "credentials" obtained through these contests to try and influence their future publication value and even their future marketability to the MFA job market. The MFA programs buy into this marketability and are even beginning to ask for this type of information on résumés, as do some magazines. What should matter is the poem and only the poem.

In *Twenty Questions*, J. D. McClatchy quotes Cyril Connolly as saying: "The true writer has only one function: To write a masterpiece. Anything less—any partial appeal—marks that writer as bogus" (49). Great poetry is going to be great no matter what and should be judged on those merits alone, not on the socio-economic status or the sexual habits, or livestock ownership of the poet, the number of contests won, or even the number of previous publications. It is this type

---

5   Personal experience.

of limiting value that has absolutely nothing to do with the poem itself which keeps new or fresh voices from coming to the forefront and poetry dangerously teetering on the bank of a stagnate pond of mediocrity.

CHAPTER THREE *prose or poetry?*

May the poetry of your love never turn to prose.

—Robert Stone, *Dog Soldiers*

"How do I know which form to put my writing in, poetry or prose?" asked a student at the 1997 summer session of the Vermont MFA program, as she had been accepted into both the prose and the poetry programs. The answer, after much debate by the panel of teachers, was that the work would seek its own form as she wrote. [6] This is indicative of the confusion surrounding the perceived gap between prose and poetry and, more importantly, the fact that most contemporary American poetry cannot be distinguished from flat prose: "The poetic has thus made an odd marriage with the prosaic, and it is this parasitic weakening of the subjective idea by an aimless prosaic experimentalism that we see in much new verse" (Kinzie 1).

Paul Valéry wrote about poetry and prose being akin to dancing and walking. Prose is like walking in that its objective is to get to a different location, the means is not relevant. Poetry, on the other hand, is likened to dance because it is

---

6 Personal experience.

the dance itself that matters, existing without an agenda. (70) Wordsworth notes: "Verse will be read a hundred times where the prose is read once" (Wordsworth 941).

Contemporary American poetry does not approach this definition. Most poems can be tolerated only once and then when the neat or catchy little image or idea is revealed, it is no longer necessary nor desirable to read the poem again. When the idea, rather than the language, remains in one's head, it is a sign that contemporary American poetry is simply prose masquerading in a costume of verse, as John Hollander states: "But most contemporary verse (and this has been true on every day since the invention of printing, at least) is not poetry" (161).

If one looks at poetry and prose as two opposing hyperbolas approaching a common axis on the great graph of literaria, then one can imagine how increasingly close these lines have come to blurring into one, solid, indiscernible mass. This does not mean that each hyperbola does not retain its respective portion of the graph as its own, but it does mean that this union has been pushed from both sides of the graph as close as it possibly can without the conjunctive intercourse of birthing a new genre.

As suggested by Edmund Wilson in "Is Verse a Dying Technique?," it is important to define the general terms of "prose," "poetry," and "verse" before proceeding in a discussion about their relationship to one another. The term "poetry" has historically been assigned to any rhymed, rhythmical, or otherwise identifiable work written in verse. "Verse," as suggested by the definition of "poetry," could superficially be considered interchangeable with the term "poetry." However, "verse" should be more accurately defined as a writing technique characterized by metrical lines, stanzas, and line breaks. A metrical line then is always considered "verse," but not necessarily considered poetry: "Verse being but an ornament and no cause to poetry [...]" (Sidney 27). Subsequently, the term "poetry," then, is open to further interpretation. "Prose," on the other hand, is assigned to any work that does not have meter or discernable rhyme and is generally characterized by paragraphs rather than line breaks (Wilson 15).

Verse has been approaching prose since its inception. As Edmund Wilson points out: "The technique of prose is inevitably tending more and more to take over the material which had formerly provided the subjects for compositions in verse [...]" (21). This statement is similar to looking at death as always beginning at birth. Is verse dying as Wilson would have us believe, or is it achieving a state of perfection through the physical appearance of death? The preceding metaphor of a geometrical graph is a balanced equation: Just as verse has been approaching prose, prose has also been approaching verse. Prose has not had the same concerns as verse because it has been going from apparent disorder to order, while, superficially at least, verse appears to have been in a general state of atrophy.

Verse has responded to this regression by socially withdrawing itself into the ramparts of ivory towers. This entrenchment in the American university has made verse virtually inaccessible to the average reader, as most poets only strive to impress fellow poets and literary critics. This vicious cycle, according to Joseph Epstein, has been exacerbated in the last two decades by the phenomenon of the MFA programs. These programs have served to further entrench verse into the university setting by allowing many poets to do nothing but write and teach thereby transporting them from the real to the surreal world. MFA programs also have dramatically increased the number of "professional" poets and even "amateur" poets being produced and sent off into publication. Dana Gioia, in his book *Can Poetry Matter?*, attributes the resultant mediocrity with driving away most readers, while Robert Bly quoted by Gioia in the same essay states that "the country is full of young poets and readers who are confused by seeing mediocre poetry praised, or never attacked [...]" (qtd. in Gioia 8). William Packard often tells the story of when Karl Shapiro asked him how many poems were published each year in *The New York Quarterly*. Packard's answer of 300 prompted Shapiro to question whether 300 good poems were written each year (Packard, "Interview").

Karl Shapiro's *Poetry Wreck*, Dana Gioia's *Can Poetry Matter?*, Edmund Wilson's "Is Verse a Dying Technique?," and Joseph Epstein's "Who Killed Poetry?" are all dedicated to the question of what has happened to poetry over the last several decades. None offer a definitive answer. They do share a few points which can offer some insight into the apparent decline of poetry's role. Poetry's readership has become largely university based. The number of "amateur" poets producing admittedly mediocre verse is dramatically increasing. This occurrence of mass quantities of verse flooding the poetry market stems not only from the workshop and MFA phenomenon but also from the type of poetry that is being generated. Verse has pulled back into its lyrical shell as a reaction to feeling inadequate next to prose. Short, metaphorically based poems, often deeply imagistic, are the current staple of most modern verse. The rest of the workshop-based attempts at narrative or prose poems generally results in poor prose that has been trimmed to look like lyric verse. These workshop poems also degenerate from a confessional or personal point of view that takes on pressing societal issues such as "the new house in Westchester" or "Prozac."

In his essay, "Is Verse a Dying Technique?" Wilson quotes Edgar Allan Poe as predicting that "no very long poem would ever be popular again" (qtd. in Wilson 18). Wilson explains this prediction when he writes "that verse as a technique was then passing out of fashion in every department of literature except those of lyric poetry and the short idyll" (18). Poe was correct in his prediction; this is our current station. Historically, though, there has been a movement to advance the use of verse by pushing it ever so close to prose. Flaubert and Baudelaire pushed these limits in the 1800s; Whitman was the first to predict this progression toward prose within the "American" language, which would not be fully recognized until the turn of the twentieth century, when Eliot and Pound would demand it, although they did not write in "American." Others who did, such as William Carlos Williams and Robert Frost would eventually only be relatively successful at pushing their verse closer to prose.

In his defense of poetry, Sidney states clearly: "It is not rhyming and versing that maketh poesy. One may be a poet without versing, and a versifier without poetry" (50). Looking in *The Longman Dictionary of Poetic Terms*, one can find the two terms "poetic prose" and "prose poetry." *Longman's* uses these two terms to better delineate the two hyperbola as they race toward one another, approaching the blur. Poetic prose is not just "really good prose," but prose exhibiting some characteristics of verse while still remaining for the most part prose: "Prose itself when it is fused with emotion becomes rhythmic, and the rhythm in turn heightens the emotional effect" (A. Lowell 10). Prose poetry, on the other hand, is not "really bad poetry," but rather verse showing some qualities of prose while retaining its general features as verse (Myers and Simms 236, 244–245).

> The prose poem can be thought of as a kind of "last genre," proposing to unite two of the basic categories of literature that have remained as distinct sparring partners since ancient Greece [...]. The prose poem hovers at the edge of this precipice, however, caught in a paradoxical situation: It has survived for a century, now, as the codification of a moment of generic dissolution, and, especially in France, has become another genre within the purview of the lyric poem. (Fredman 5)

Some of these mingling qualities would include spatial versus temporal form, syllabic rhythm compared to a phrasing-based rhythm, and the origination of the line break as either metrical or syntactical.

Contemporary American poets seem confused as to what exactly sets poetry apart from prose. Often "identified only by their jagged right-hand edge, [...]" (Hollander 6) most contemporary American poems are no more than a prose divided into line breaks. Some poets only see the use of verse as a throwback to the songwriter and the use of the line break as mere scaffolding, a unit in which to work (McPherson 58). If one were to take an anthology such as Jack Myers and Roger Weingarten's *New American Poets of the '90s*, it would be easy to arbitrarily open the book to a poem, remove all the line breaks, and expose the dreadfully flat prose. As a matter of fact, it would be too easy, too convenient to state that the removal of the line breaks is the sole delineating factor. The degradation of a poetic verse into a prose with line breaks has been warned against repeatedly by critics:

> Do not retell in mediocre verse what has already been done in good prose. Don't think any intelligent person is going to be deceived when you try to shirk all the difficulties of the unspeakably difficult art of good prose by chopping your composition into line lengths. (Pound, *Essays* 5)

This danger becomes especially acute in free verse, as warned by T.S. Eliot in his essay "Reflections on 'Vers Libre'": "[In Vers Libre] the lines are usually explicable in terms of prosody. Any line can be divided into feet and accents" (Eliot 32). Amy Lowell agrees with Eliot, but explains it further:

> *Vers libre* looks easy to write, and bad *vers libre* is easy; but when it is bad it is not *vers libre* at all, but prose cut into arbitrary lines. The lines of good *vers libre* are not arbitrary, they are determined by the interrelating circles of the rhythm. (70)

Unfortunately, as the years progressed away from Modernism, these warnings have been forgotten. With each successive generation of poets, the integrity of the line has been increasingly neglected. Much of this can be blamed on free verse giving the illusion of ease of composition. When poets simply mock other poets of the same age or, at best, poets of a previous generation, the use of the line becomes like a photocopy of a photocopy—the "Xerox syndrome." The integrity that may have been present in the original has increasingly faded with every successive generation.

Donald Hall addresses the removal of the line break:

> When a critic takes a lined poem and prints it as prose, in order to show that the poem is inferior, he tells us nothing about the poem. [...] Such a critic reveals that he is ignorant or disingenuous. [...] They [those during the early wars over free verse] only proved that they had no sense of the line. (Hall, "The Line" 74)

Ezra Pound, of course, held onto the notion of the musical phrase within the line. However, one of the first contemporary defining characteristics of the free verse line was noted by Charles Olson in his essay "Projective Verse." In this essay, he introduces the possibility that the length of the line is determined by the natural breath of a person:

> For the first time the poet has the stave and the bar a musician has had. For the first time he can, without the convention of rime and meter, record the listening he has done to his own speech and by that one act indicate how he would want any reader, silently or otherwise, to voice his work. (154)

John Haines expands upon this idea: "I learned to break the lines in some pattern, visual or other, and to make some effective use of the phrase as the language is spoken, or as I speak it myself. And all this has been very largely a matter of instinct" (69). Relying on instinct alone, however, has led us to the point we are: Copies of copies, the "Xerox syndrome."

If one relies on instinct, then one is relying on both what one has read and other influences in one's life: "Tendencies, familiar to poets from memories—conscious and unconscious—of reading poems, are among the many factors influencing their decisions about lines" (Matthews 78). As shown in an earlier chapter, contemporary poets fail to take risks in life or even live in life, so that part of the influence is dry. We also know from Stewardship (see Chapter 5) that the influence of other people's work on contemporary poets is limited to their teachers and classmates, which leads us right back to the "Xerox syndrome."

Ultimately, though, the line is most definitely a unit of rhythm; a point most contemporary poets forget: "Prose has no prosody. And poetry—though it may not tick like a metronome or decorate nor inflate, must make music" (Plumly I: 24). Louis Simpson incorporates these concepts of breath and influence and rhythm into the following statement:

> The line is a unit of rhythm. The poet is moved by impulses of rhythm which he expresses in lines of verse. Impulse determines where each line breaks, and the impulse of the poem as a whole determines the look of the poem on the page or its sound in the air. (68–69)

Therefore, the line break determinations are a combination of several factors, most of which revert directly back to the inward state of the poet:

> The decision to break lines at this or that point, to arrange them in whatever form or pattern, comes from the direction of the energy or impulse of the poet. This energy, this

emotional charge, is going to change, to swerve, to rise and fall, to hurry and then relax from time to time, from poem to poem, or from moment to moment. Changes of line have a lot to do with changes in the poet's life; it's an internal affair as well as an outward, or technical decision to write this way or that. And if you find yourself becoming restricted by your own style, then you must change it. But first you must change your life. (Haines 70)

If contemporary American poetry used strict form, then the definition of the line would be predisposed, but most contemporary American poetry is not in traditional form; it is in free verse.[7] These definitions demonstrate the fuzzy use of the line break in free verse. Because of this fuzziness, a clear-cut definition can not be applied across the board. Therefore, a definitive test must be used that will allow for the examination of each individual use of the line. As Charles Wright observes: "There are writers who compose their lined poems sentence by sentence. Such poems have a prosey ring to my ear" (172). In poems constructed in this manner it is possible to remove a line break from the poem and the absence will not be noticed. As already shown, however, the poem with appropriate line breaks is tied to the innermost essence of the poet; therefore, it is as organic as the poet themselves. The acid test, then, for determining a proper use of the line break is its relationship to the whole:

One cannot take one line, one scene, one figure, one measure from its place and put it in some other place without

---

7   It should be acknowledged that in the sense of form, Free Verse itself is now considered traditional.

disturbing the meaning of the whole, just as one cannot but disturb the life of an organic being by taking an organ from its place and putting it somewhere else. (Tolstoy 103)

This sentiment is echoed by Haines: "And once written, the poem intends to stay fiercely in its form; it resists change. I don't understand this, it's mysterious like everything else that is important in poetry" (70). And Horace emphatically states: "So make what you like, provided the thing is a unified whole" (23).

Therefore, if the line break can be removed and the poem not lose an iota of sound or sense, then the verse in question is simply prose and not poetry. The initial test discussed of removing the line breaks and placing the verse into a paragraph then stands as a valid test of poetry.

The line break in contemporary American poetry also plays a part in an even greater function than that of identifying poetic verse: "It seems to me that lineation nearly always contributes to the tension of a work, if only because it is doled out to the reader one line at a time" (McPherson 63). Poetry needs prose to push against.

Energy is created as an electron shifts between the orbits of an atom. The energy eminates from that change, that tension. Similarly, Charles Wright describes poetry as it journeys out of prose and creates a tension of resisting the return to that prose. It is in this tension and the "journey up and back, [which] is more charged, more filled with meaning, and that's where poetry resides" (Wright 136–138).

Much like a water spider, it is this delicate surface tension that keeps poetry afloat and when poets lose this tension they begin to sink into the quagmire of the prosaic:

> When the traditional, metrical, sonic means of foreground-
> ing the verbal surface of verse is not available, a poet will
> turn, instinctively almost to semantic means: stock lines
> with metaphors and similes. As if to compensate in the
> domain of the "sense" what he has given up in the domain
> of sound. (Holden, *Fate* 93 – 94)

In his essay "The Serious Artist," Ezra Pound states he "believe[s] that poetry is the more highly energized. But these things are relative.[…] The thing that counts is 'Good writing'" (*Literary Essays* 49). Pound continues to explain that "Good writing is writing that is perfectly controlled, the writer says just what he means" (49). Pound emphasizes not only in this essay but also in the *ABC of Reading* that "Great Literature is simply language charged with meaning to the utmost pos-sible degree" (36).

As Charles Bukowski once wrote, " I slide back and forth between those two prosties (sic), prose und (sic) poem, I don't know why more people don't give themselves relief like that" (14). This brings us back to the original observation of the woman at the Vermont MFA program who did not know which genre in which to write. The question is not between poetry and prose, the question is between verse and prose. If one writes with a charged language then: "Every form is proper to poetry, so long as it is the sincere expression of a man's thought" (A. Lowell 7).

Edmund Wilson answers his own question regarding the fate of "poetry":

Is it not time to discard the word 'poetry' or to define it in such a way as to take account of the fact that the most intense, the most profound, the most beautifully composed and the most comprehensive of the great works of literary art (which for these reasons are also the most thrilling and give us most prickly sensations while shaving) have been written sometimes in verse technique, sometimes in prose technique, depending partly on the taste of the author, partly on the mere current fashion. It is only when we argue these matters that we become involved in absurdities. (21)

Therefore, poetry is not dead nor is it dying, it is in the act of achieving a heavenly perfection. As verse approaches prose in its constructs and the two forms become blurred, it is important to remember that it is the poets themselves who keep that razor's edge tension between poetry and prose sharp and definable. It is from the innermost depths of the poet that the language receives its charge. The delineating factor between poetry and prose is the sacrifice of the self: Poetry is being.

CHAPTER FOUR *the muse*

In order to speak, the poet, too, listens.

—J. D. McClatchy, *White Paper*

At a reading in New York City given by Nicholas Christopher and Charles Simic, the "3 A.M. in the morning poem" was not only described as an inferior poem compared to one that is crafted, but it was repeatedly derided by both the presenters and the audience. When asked which was more important, the craft or Muse, Charles Simic made the choice of craft.[8] An ever expanding mentality of poetic production has virtually removed the concept of the Muse from the poetic process— an emphasis which is in direct opposition to both historical poets and critics alike who have always had reverence for the Muse. The inversion of emphasis between craft and the Muse has arisen out of the creative writing workshops and MFA programs as an effort to demystify the writing process so that poetry writing can be taught in a formulaic manner (Grimes 19). The removal of the Muse from poetry is one of the main factors, if not *the* main factor, which sets contemporary American poetry apart from its predecessors and

_____

8   Personal observation.

contributes to its mediocrity. The answer that Charles Simic should have given was that neither craft nor Muse was more or less important.

Within the American university there is an ever-increasing pressure on both teachers and students to "perform" by publishing books of poetry. Most creative writing teaching jobs place emphasize on "substantial publication" or "significant creative publication" as a prerequisite for even an initial consideration of a teaching candidate.[9] The reasoning behind this aspect is obvious. First, it is a convenient weed-out factor. Much like standardized testing, whoever conforms in the academic community by having the most published, gets the job. This removes the burden of the hiring committee to select candidates based on their inherent skill as poets:

> Poets serious about making careers in institutions understand that the criteria for success are primarily quantitative. They must publish as much as possible as quickly as possible. The slow maturation of genuine creativity looks like laziness to a committee. (Gioia 9)

Once the job is attained, however, another side effect of affiliating with an academic institution exists, in which "writers must, of course, just like their more scholarly colleagues, publish as much and as widely as possible to keep their jobs, to gain tenure, to earn merit raises, and so forth" (Garrett 57). Secondly, the publication record of the teacher is tied directly to that teacher's fame. This is as an added benefit necessary for the MFA program because it not only draws potential

---

9   As evidenced by perusing any AWP job list.

students, but also provides for potential publication connections for the students (Shelnutt 16).

It is the publication of the student that is of utmost importance to the MFA program. This importance is imposed, not simply because this is the implied guarantee to every student enrolled, but because the fiscal existence of the program is dependent upon it:

> Student publication as an indicator of a program's health is something I have not heard debated among writing teachers as being, possibly, a two-sided issue. Nor is it likely to be debated as long as MFA programs advertise their programs by touting student publication. [...] Nevertheless, students are pressured to publish: Publication will ensure renewal of a fellowship, help the writing program advertise itself, and possibly open the doors to New York. (Shelnutt 17–18)

The poet adapts in order to meet this publish-or-perish necessity. The assimilation of the poet to mass production of work begins in the workshop. Requiring the production of a poem or poems on a weekly basis, students quickly learn to produce rather than to gestate their ideas: "The imperative in a workshop is to create an atmosphere where poets are encouraged to write, not wait for the urgency of having something to say (the point is to be ready when that moment comes)" (Altieri 206). Soon, all that remains is the crafting of an idea, sans inspiration. Donald Hall observes that: "If we learn one thing else, we learn to publish promiscuously: These premature ejaculations count on number and frequency to counterbalance ineptitude" ("Ambition" 239). With the crafting of poetry in the forefront, poets become mere assembly line technicians cranking out formulaic poetry on a daily basis in order to maintain their academic positions by counting coup on publication "badges of honor": "Poetry is not like reasoning, a power to be exerted according to the determination of the will. A man cannot say, 'I will compose poetry'" (Shelley 503).

In this process, poetry, deprived of the Muse, is scalped with superficial renderings, unenlightening epiphanies, and an epidemic avoidance of self-exploration. In *Can Poetry Matter?* Dana Gioia says: "A poetry industry has been created to serve the interests of the producers and not the consumers. And in the process the integrity of the art has been betrayed" (10). The practice of scheduling time in one's office to write a poem, squeezed between faculty meetings, classes, or office hours has poets churning out poems about the clocks in their offices rather than about life experiences that have affected their innermost selves. Placing the Muse in the background removes the influence of the unconscious and the inner self, and, therefore removes the "soul" of the poet from poetry. The resulting poetry created becomes mediocre at best.

Longinus likened the Muse to the "Pythian priestess at Delphi, when she approaches the tripod at the place where there is a cleft in the ground, is said to inhale a divine vapor; thus at once she becomes impregnated with divine power and, suddenly inspired, she utters oracles" (22). Plato also addressed the infection of the Muse in "Ion":

> And the soul of the lyric poet does the same, as they themselves say; for they tell us that they bring songs from honeyed fountains culling them out of the gardens and dells

of the Muses; they, like the bees, winging their way from flower to flower. And this is true. For the poet is a light and winged and holy thing [...]. (1: 289)

In his book, *American Poetry: Wildness and Domesticity*, Robert Bly recalls an ancient time of inspiration in China where poets "flew from one world to another, 'riding on dragons'[...][dragging] behind them long tails of dragon smoke" (42). No matter how you choose to think of the Muse, once removed from the art of poetry, contemplation has been removed; removing contemplation removes the self, and once that has been removed from the poetic voice, the poem becomes soulless.

The Muses of ancient Greece were seen as the influence upon a poet or artist by one of nine demi-goddesses: Calliope, epic poetry; Clio, history; Euterpe, music; Terpsichore, lyric poetry/dancing; Erato, lyric poetry; Melpomene, tragedy; Thalia, comedy; Polyhymnia, hymns; and Urania, astronomy. Their father being Zeus, the Muses are unmistakably connected to memory through their mother, Mnemosyne, the goddess of memory (Hesiod 126–127; "Muses"):

If the art of concentrating in a particular way is the discipline necessary for poetry to reveal itself, memory exercised in a particular way is the natural gift of poetic genius. The poet, above all else, is a person who never forgets certain sense-impressions which he has experienced and which he can relive again and again as though with all their original freshness. (Spender 55)

Believing the Muses would write through the poet is a

common explanation in classical literature for creative inspiration (externally inspired, they believed). Many religious practitioners today believe that this method was used by God writing through the authors of the Judeo-Christian Bible, thus the dogmatic belief in its Divine Inspiration. Today, however, most critics and poets disregard an actual amanuensis as J. D. McClatchy quotes John Ashbery as saying: "Of course, my reason tells me that my poems are not dictated, that I am not a voyant. I suppose they come from a part of me that I am not in touch with very much except when I am writing" (*White Paper* 46).

The term "Muse" comes from the French, *musen*, to gape or stare (with an open mouth), by way of the Latin, *mūsa*, and the Greek, μοῦσα (*mousa*), meaning "to think, remember" ("Muse"). The Muse is likened to inspiration by Denise Levertov:

> To contemplate comes from "*templum*, temple, a place, a space for observation, marked out by the augur." It means, not simply to observe, to regard, but to do these things in the presence of a god. And to meditate is "to keep the mind in a state of contemplation"; its synonym is "to muse," and to muse comes from a word meaning "to stand with open mouth"—not so comical if we think of "inspiration"—to breathe in. (68–69)

The inspiration received from the Muses, then, comes only after practicing the inward art of contemplation.

Contemplation requires two main stages in order to be successfully accomplished: feeding and gestation. The feeding of the Muse comes not only from constant reading and study but also from constantly observing both man and nature: "The poet's mind is in fact a receptacle for seizing and storing up numberless feelings, phrases, images, which remain there until all the particles which can unite to form a new compound are present together" (Eliot 41). This is why what the poet reads, studies, and experiences are all a part of the input to their poetry; to use the old cliché, "You are what you eat." One's poems become what one digests into their psyche. This is why stewardship, discussed in the next chapter, is so very important. If one restricts one's reading to only contemporary American poetry, then one has no choice but to write like other contemporary American poets. As well, if one leads a "safe" life of hiding behind the ramparts of academia, then that is all one will know to write about. This is the same reasoning behind why a ten-year-old boy singing his heart out about love and loss is just not believable; he has not experienced it for real.

The gestation phase is the second half of the contemplation process. As Rainer Maria Rilke states in his *Letters to a Young Poet*, "*Everything* is gestation and then birthing" (23). Inspiration arises out of contemplation. Without both phases of contemplation, however, inspiration does not manifest. Gestation cannot be forced, which makes it the most frustrating and difficult part of contemplation to bear:

> For poesy must not be drawn by the ears; it must be gently led, or rather it must lead—which was partly the cause that made the ancient-learned affirm it was a divine gift, and no human skill: Since all other knowledges lie ready for any that hath strength of wit. (Sidney 63)

This aspect of contemplation requires not only tremendous patience, but also great fortitude to suffer through the dry, uninspired spells. The Muse can go as quickly as it comes. Not only can the poet suffer through dry spells, there is also an ephemeral nature to the state of the Muse as it reveals itself to the poet:

> Poetry, like so much else that is beautiful, is ephemeral. A butterfly, a nightingale, a sip of wine. It slips away, the particular joining the general. How many marvelously apt haikus have been written—and lost before the sun came up? Several million at least. Any poet must be prepared to see his work arise and vanish in the same morning mists. (Disch 34)

Take for instance the famous story behind Samuel Taylor Coleridge's composition of *Kubla Kahn*:

> In 1797, while living near the Wordsworths in Somerset, Coleridge took opium and fell asleep when reading a passage in *Purchas his Pilgrimage* […], relating to the Khan Kubla and the palace that he commanded to be built. On awaking he was conscious of having composed in his sleep two or three hundred lines on this theme and eagerly began to set down the lines that form this fragment. He was then interrupted by a 'person…from Porlock,' and, on returning to his task an hour later, found that almost the entire remainder of the poem had slipped from his memory. ("Kubla Khan")

The Muse has historically manifested itself in dreams or during times of illness, extreme mental anguish ("the poet needing the pain"), and during drug or alcohol use. All of these instances of its manifestation have one thing in common: The breaking down of the barrier between the conscious and the unconscious. "It would seem that a scientific definition of a poet might put it something like this: A man of an extraordinarily sensitive and active subconscious personality, fed by, and feeding, a nonresistant consciousness" (A. Lowell 25).

The most accessible insight that the poet has into the unconscious is through dreams:

> Thus the esthetically sensitive man stands in the same relation to the reality of dreams as the philosopher does to the reality of existence; he is a close and willing observer, for these pictures afford him an interpretation of life, and it is by these processes that he trains himself for life. (Nietzsche 2)

It is the flux between these two primary processes of waking and sleeping which opens the window onto the unconscious. Using a Jakobson-influenced model of Freud's psychic processes, Christopher Collins places manifest dreaming as a primary process of the sleeping state closest to the line of waking. Therefore, as dreams arise out of the unconscious closest to the time of waking, their images transcend from the unconscious to the waking conscious. This is why it is important to jot down dreams immediately after waking. The converse can also hold true in that the primary process of waking thought lies just on the waking side of the line between sleeping and waking; therefore, any influence on the waking, primary process that depresses consciousness across the threshold into the realm of sleeping—alcohol, depressants, psychological problems, fatigue—immediately becomes a window into the unconscious through visions or daydreams (Collins, "Lecture").[10]

In his 1924 "Manifesto," André Breton attempts to tap into this interplay: "I believe in the future resolution of these two states, dream and reality, which are seemingly so contradictory, into a kind of absolute reality, a *surreality*, if one may so speak" (14). It is Breton's concept of this surreality that gave us automatic writing and the entire Surrealist movement.

The key to these dream processes is the delving into the unconscious: A removal of inhibitions and filters that exist in the conscious mind. Once these inhibitions have been removed, the Muse is free to inspire:

> The idea of Surrealism aims quite simply at the total recovery of our psychic force by a means which is nothing other than the dizzying descent into ourselves, the systematic illumination of hidden places and the progressive darkening of other places, the perceptual excursion into the midst of forbidden territory. (Breton 136 –137)

Therefore, the Muse exists out of that part of ourselves that we keep in our unconscious and must allow ourselves to descend into that area of ourselves and summon the Muse.

The Muse, however, does not stand alone in the creation of poetry. Just as in the example given to us by Coleridge, it takes more than the Muse to make a poet. Equally as important as the Muse is the other half of the equation—craft.

---

10   This topic is, of course, far too detailed to cover in the context of this thesis. It also does not exclude the Jungian theory of the collective unconscious, but this, too, is far too in-depth for our purposes here.

Without technical crafting of what the Muse has provided, great poetry is not created:

> Is it a gift or a craft that makes outstanding poetry? I fail, myself, to see the good either of study without a spark of genius or of untutored talent. Each requires the other's help in a common cause. (Horace 408–411)

As seen in Longinus' five sources of great poetry, the first two in the list arise out of the Muse while the last three arise out of craft (10).[11] These two must go hand in hand:

> Here is where the conscious training of the poet comes in, for he must fill in what the subconscious has left, and fill it in as much in the key of the rest as possible. [...] Hence the innumerable rewritings which poems undergo. [...] This is the reason that a poet must be both born and made. He must be born with a subconscious factory always working for him or he never can be a poet at all, and he must have knowledge and talent enough to 'putty up' his holes [...]. (A. Lowell 26–27)

But craft cannot stand alone. Denise Levertov sounds a warning to those who would ignore the Muse:

> To believe, as an artist, in *inspiration* or *the intuitive*, to

---

11 According to Longinus the five sources of great writing are:
1) Vigor of mental conception.
2) Strong and inspired emotion.
3) Adequate fashioning of figures.
4) Nobility of diction.
5) Dignified and distinguished word arrangement.

know that without Imagination (and I give it the initial capital in conscious allusion to Keats's famous dictum) no amount of acquired craft or scholarship or of brilliant reasoning will suffice, is to live with a door of one's life open to the transcendent, the numinous. Not every artist, clearly, acknowledges that fact—yet all, in the creative act, experience mystery. (241)

This warning rings true and clear after understanding that MFA programs teach craft without the Muse, resulting in mediocrity.

Charles Bukowski sums up the issue of the Muse in a very practical and down to earth way when he says, "Don't try" (21). This infamous epigraph was his view on both life and writing poetry. Just let it happen, don't force it, don't try: "I dislike rules, they are made to be broken. But I'd say the best thing to go by is—never write unless you really *feel* like writing, it has to come out like hot turds the morning after a good beer drunk" (54).

Bukowski saw forcing a poem as artificial and leading to mediocrity: "Poetry, most of it, is so dull because it's so practiced" (169). Poets who solely focus on craft and ignore the Muse completely abandon all that might be available to them through the unconscious, thereby successfully avoiding exploration of their innermost selves and personal voice.

CHAPTER FIVE *stewardship*

We shall not cease from exploration
And the end of all our exploration
Will be to arrive where we started
And know the place for the first time.

—T. S. Eliot, *Four Quartets*

Newton's Third Law of Motion states that for every action there is an equal and opposite reaction. It then follows that the stronger the action, the stronger the reaction. In his book *From Modern to Contemporary*, James E. B. Breslin quotes Theodore Roethke: "A poet is judged, in part, by the influences he resists" (qtd. in Breslin 5). A swimmer stands poised ready to dive. Before taking that plunge, however, he must first push off against the edge of the pool in order to gain distance and form entering the water. At that moment in time, between the push and the splash, exists the poet. The poet must have the solid tradition to push against and a large enough pool in which to dive. The poet must be cognizant at all times of both the ground and the pool, for if they exist solely in the present, all the training and practice cannot help the poet avoid making a big belly flop into a shallow pool: "We don't live merely in the present. There is a past, and there is and will be a future. Out of nothing comes nothing. Maybe we need faith more than anything else" (Haines 72). Stewardship exists through a certain point in time, a point in time that will never be the same again: It is always defined by an ever changing past and future.

Many poets today fear that reading poets of the past will somehow inhibit their own sensibilities: an "anxiety of influence." This myth is sustained by the curriculum of MFA programs which require the reading of a full complement of contemporary poets while at best, only allowing a lean diet of the classics. If one reads only contemporary poets, then one only writes like contemporary poets—not in one's own unique voice.

For our purposes here, a classic is defined as that of the western canon. However, in defining the classics of literature it should be made clear: "A classic is a classic not because it conforms to certain structural rules, or fits certain definitions (of which its author had quite probably never heard). It is classic because of a certain eternal and irrepressible freshness" (Pound, *ABC* 13–14). A classic, then, can be anything from the western canon or, for the member of a culture with no written tradition, the oral tradition.

Much of this "anxiety of influence" stems from a fear of not being original in one's work. But originality is often misunderstood by burgeoning writers who mistakenly import an anxiety surrounding this need for originality into their work. It is the anxiety instilled by a literary tradition that is this fallacy of originality which drives writers to develop gimmicky techniques and superficial craft instead of developing their own voice: "The covert subject of most poetry for the last three centuries has been the anxiety of influence, each poet's fear that no proper work remains for him to perform" (Bloom, *Anxiety* 148). By examining this "anxiety of influence" closely and with an open mind, one can discover that the legacy of the past helps rather than hinders the development of an original voice.

The grand irony of the anxiety of influence is that it comes to us via the literary tradition. In recent times, most critics (including Bloom) place the resurgence of the originality question with the Romantics: "In essence, what [Roland] Motier contends is that with the advent of Romantic literary theory in England, Germany, and France, the concept of *originality* in and of itself became a distinct aesthetic category or criterion for both the creation and appreciation of literary works" (Metzidakis 29).

Since the Romantics, however, there have been numerous movements making a break with tradition, including the avant-garde, free verse (Whitman), and the Beats. Each of these movements was a reactive attempt to break from tradition and redefine the writing of poetry. A reaction necessarily implies a knowledge of an action (as exemplified in the opening paragraph). How can one break free from something if it is not known what that something is? No one can:

> At such moments of redefinition, however, there are complicating factors at work. What is involved, after all, is the replacement of ideas of literary excellence derived from modes of expression originally taken to be canonical and unquestionable. Writers have to start out as readers, and before they put pen to paper, even the most disaffected of them will have internalized the norms and forms of the tradition from which they wish to secede. (Heaney 6)

Therefore, these movements were breaking from tradition by working within the knowledge of that previous tradition.

However, in this Postmodern age, poets are breaking from the past by neglecting the tradition altogether, reacting by not pushing against the side of the pool; therefore, they are belly-flopping. As Karl Shapiro once observed: "The downhill speed of American Poetry in the last decade has been breathtaking, for those who watch the sport. Poetry plunged out of the classics, out of the modern masters, out of all standards, and plopped into the playpen" (*Poetry Wreck* 360). And as Thomas M. Disch has observed about most workshop students: "No sense of the history embedded in their own tongue. Even in their own language they will have read only a smattering of its classics, and they will have been taught to dismiss most of that as fusty, patristic, and irrelevant […]" (8).

When applying to the Vermont College MFA, then director Roger Weingarten instructed this author to read as many contemporary poets as possible—and only contemporary poets. It eventually became clear that this was characteristic of many MFA programs and creative writing workshops and not just confined to the Vermont College MFA.

Removing the classics from the instruction of poetry and focusing solely on the study of contemporary poets limits the knowledge and breadth of the poet. In order to survive and grow, the Muse must be fed. Just as our bodies "are what we eat," so the Muse becomes what the poet feeds it through reading. By digesting a variety of works representative of the history of literature, the poet inhales those divine vapors referred to by Longinus. Then the Muse provides a platform from which the poet can develop a distinctive voice and further advance that same literary history.

Ignoring the literary tradition does not make it go away;

rather, the tradition languishes like an unwatered plant. Writers who deny this literary tradition are doomed to not know their own history: "And he is not likely to know what is to be done unless he lives in what is not merely the present, but the present moment of the past, unless he is conscious, not of what is dead, but of what is already living" (Eliot 44). Only by recognizing this tradition, learning it and breaking from it is progress made. Learning only the most recent poets and depriving oneself of adopting a full literary tradition, the contemporary poet has no option but to write like every other MFA student. This can be proven by lining up a series of books from any MFA program, by students and teachers alike, and searching for individual voices. The unique voice of a poet which might have been heard prior to his or her enrollment in an MFA program becomes like the fourth generation offspring of the only French Poodle in a town full of hound dogs: The puppies start to look more like hound dogs than French Poodles. A distinct voice does not exist. Rather, a collective voice characteristic of that particular school begins to emerge, patterned solely after the limited influences of that school's teaching staff:

> It is so clear to most critics and teachers of poetry that the workshop tends to produce certain kinds of poetry and not others. [...] The workshop as it exists in most American universities not only tends to homogenize the level of what has traditionally constituted authorial style—substituting a notion of personal "voice" or "authenticity" for more inventive linguistic or stylistic manipulation—but it also tends to breed a conformity to certain established patterns of verse, in particular the self-contained, narrative,

lyric, first-person poems that have dominated mainstream
American poetry for the past twenty years. (Beach 14)

Ideally in creative writing workshops, the student is
taught not only by the teacher, but also by all the people who
influenced that teacher (Wright 54). However, with much of
the teaching staff just graduating from other MFA programs
themselves, the student's experience is limited solely to
the contemporary writers who influenced the teachers, the
teachers themselves, and their immediate peers (Garrett 59).
Couple this with the fact that the students only read contemporary poetry written by their peers, teachers or "those
with whom their instructors network," the circle of isolation
becomes complete (Disch 9).

By writing within a literary tradition, the poet makes the
past contemporaneous, making the poets of a thousand years
ago seem like best friends who share work interchangeably.
T. S. Eliot refers to this as the "historical sense":

> Tradition is a matter of much wider significance. It cannot
> be inherited, and if you want it you must obtain it by great
> labour. It involves, in the first place, the historical sense,
> which we may call nearly indispensable to anyone who
> would continue to be a poet beyond his twenty-fifth year;
> and the historical sense involves a perception, not only of
> the pastness of the past, but of its presence; the histori-
> cal sense compels a man to write not merely with his own
> generation in his bones, but with a feeling that the whole
> of the literature of Europe from Homer and within it the
> whole of literature of his own country has a simultaneous
> order. This historical sense, which is a sense of the time-

less as well as of the temporal and of the timeless and the temporal together, is what makes a writer traditional. And it is at the same time what makes a writer most acutely conscious of his place in time, of his own contemporaneity. (38)

Wendell Berry expands upon this concept of contemporaneity, extending it in a direction that is diametrically opposed to both the MFA concept of an isolated contemporaneity and the concept of demystification purported by the creative writing workshop:

Contemporaneity, in the sense of being "up with the times," is of no value.[…] The job now is to get back to that other perennial and substantial world in which we really do live, in which the foundations of our life will be visible to us, and in which we can accept our responsibilities again within the conditions of necessity and mystery. In that world all competently wakeful and responsible people, dead, living, and unborn, are contemporaries. And that is the only contemporaneity worth having. (20)

It is this effect of contemporaneity, of encompassing all the tradition within one's self, that helps to develop that poet's individual voice. As Edwin Muir emphasizes: "Poetry will not truly be contemporary, or truly poetry, if it deals merely with the immediately perceived contemporary world as if that existed by itself and were isolated from all that preceded it" (92). No other poet has ever put together the same tradition in quite the same way before; each tradition becomes as individual as fingerprints. Once attained, this literary tradition is to be employed in a subtle manner within the voice of the poet: "But the difference between the present and the past is that the conscious present is an awareness of the past in a way and to an extent which the past's awareness of itself cannot show" (Eliot 39).

Eliot explains the importance of literary tradition upon individuality:

> The mind of the poet is the [...][catalyst]. It may partly or exclusively operate upon the experience of the man himself; but, the more perfect the artist, the more completely separate in him will be the man who suffers and the mind which creates; the more perfectly will the mind digest and transmute the passions which are its material. (41)

Harold Bloom's arguments are not far from those of Eliot's when distilled down to the basics:

> Both agree that originality is not so much an avoidance of influence as a special manifestation of it. Both Bloom and Eliot attempt to dissolve the antithetical relationship between originality and influence initiated by the Romantics and still to a large extent inscribed in subsequent systems of literary evaluation. (Ryan 228)

It is this sameness that is often overlooked in today's literary circles, but boiled down to the basics, Bloom is also saying that any great writer cannot avoid the anxiety of influence:

> When a potential poet first discovers (or is discovered by) the dialectic of influence, first discovers poetry as being

both external and internal to himself, he begins a process that will end only when he has no more poetry within him, long after he has the power (or desire) to discover it outside himself again. Though all such discovery is a self-recognition, indeed a Second Birth, and ought, in the pure good of theory, to be accomplished in a perfect solipsism, it is an act never completed in itself. Poetic Influence in the sense—amazing, agonizing, delighting—of *other poets*, as felt in the depths of the all but perfect solipsist, the potentially strong poet. For the poet is condemned to learn his profoundest yearnings through an awareness of *other selves*. The poem is *within* him, yet he experiences the shame and splendor of *being found by* poems—great poems—*outside* him. To lose freedom in this center is never to forgive, and to learn the dread of threatened autonomy forever. (Bloom, *Anxiety* 25–26)

But what of the individuality of the poet within tradition? The tradition cannot exist unless we allow it, and then only through our choosing and selectivity can we shape and mold the tradition to suit ourselves; this is our individuality, our poetic voice. Our minds being a *tabula rasa* at birth, one could argue that nothing has existed before us: "But in the world of imagination and of human beings all is different. There you find no consistent progress, no starting where the previous generation left off; instead there is continuity. Every human being begins at the beginning, as his fathers did [...]" (Muir 87). It is only through our manifestation of tradition that we recreate our own tradition, build on it and carry it forward to the next generation. As Harold Bloom quotes Goethe saying: "There is all this talk about originality, but what does it amount to? As soon as we are born the world begins to influence us, and this goes on till we die. And anyway, what can we in fact call our own except the energy, the force, the will!" (qtd. in *Anxiety* 52). Immediately after birth we begin to formulate our tradition, first with the recognition of our parents and the fact that they are older, then with the stories they tell. Both they and their stories become alive in us. Then as we start to read and learn, the literary tradition begins to germinate within us.

The evolutionary biological principle of "ontogeny recapitulates phylogeny" states that every organism in its gestational development mimics the evolutionary development of the species. For example, a human embryo passes through a stage where it has gills, thus representing the corresponding stage of human evolutionary development. The development of the literary tradition in each of us is similar. First, we learn through visual stimulation (cave painting), then through an oral tradition of story telling (pre-Homeric), then we begin to read and remember verse through nursery rhymes (Rhapsodic), etc. True, there is the greater tradition, which pervades all of literature no matter what we read, but developmentally we each learn our own version of the literary tradition. This becomes the filter through which we read and write.

There is, of course, the question of what happens without this filter:

> Why, nothing at all happens, just nothing. You cannot write or teach or think or even read without imitation, and what you imitate is what another person has done, that person's writing or teaching or thinking or reading. Your relation to

what informs that person is tradition, for tradition is influence that extends past one generation, a carrying-over of
influence. (Bloom, *Poetics of Influence* 109–110)

Given this, each tradition is highly individualized and
original, in and of itself. This evolutionary aspect of the literary tradition is just like any other evolutionary process: It is
infinitely slow and takes only small steps; there are no giant
leaps: "There is no success in poetry, there is only the next
inch" (Wright 102). Each inch, then, is the life of a poet, and it
is the struggle of each poet to advance the literary tradition:

I don't know how to get this new kind of sound, or this
new kind of use in language, but I am convinced that it can
be done by somebody, maybe not by me, but by somebody. I feel about myself as a writer like John the Baptist
did, when he said, "I prepare the way for one who is greater
than I." Yeah, but look who it was! (Dickey 35)

Stewardship exists as a dialectic of time between past,
present and future. All three intertwined within a triad of
timelessness. Beginning with the central core of the present,
Longinus refers to stewardship as an account for our actions
to those past and then questions how the future will receive
the present (23).

Not only is the present influenced by the past, but also
it follows that the future will be influenced by the present,
at once being measured by the past while simultaneously
becoming the measurement of the future: "For all of them
achieve a style that captures and oddly retains priority over
their precursors, so that the tyranny of time almost is over-

turned, and one can believe, for startled moments, that they are being *imitated by their ancestors*" (Bloom, *Anxiety* 141). And just as the future influences the present, the present, in turn, influences the past:

> The existing order is complete before the new work ar-
> rives; for order to persist after the supervention of novelty,
> the *whole* existing order must be, if ever so slightly, altered;
> and so the relations, proportions, values of each work of
> art toward the whole are readjusted; and this is conformity
> between the old and the new. (Eliot 38–39)

Therefore, the dialectic of stewardship is one of infinitude. Two eternal arrows passing in opposite directions through the present. And it is precisely this point in time, where these two arrows intersect with the present, that defines the precise moment for the process of poetic creation.

Ezra Pound's process was steeped in literary tradition. It was in this process that he not only developed his own voice, but also helped to define the imagistic style, which itself broke from tradition in the same manner as the Romantics. Ezra Pound's famous saying "Make it New" is often misunderstood to be a superficial call to originality. But in a true Poundian sense, it is something much deeper. It is, in fact, a phrase that embodies the timelessness of stewardship.

Pound discovered the saying when translating an inscription located on the Chinese Emperor, Ch'eng T'ang's bathtub. Ch'eng's daily admonishment given in "Canto LIII" in the original Chinese: "新日日新" (hsin, jih, jih, hsin)[12] (Pound,

---

12   Pinyin: Xin, Rih, Rih, Xin.

Cantos 265) is translated by Pound as "make new, day by day, make new." This 'spirit' of Emperor Ch'eng T'ang describes the regenerative and ethical metamorphoses effected by the Shang dynasty and functions at all neo-confucian periods in the dynastic cantos" (Terrell 1: 205). Thus, Pound is saying that every day one should strive to make all that interests one's psyche new. "Make it your own," as Jane Hirshfield interprets the phrase (11). Make the past, present and future all your own. And W. S. Merwin states: "True originality has to do not with trying to be new but trying to come from the place from which all renewal comes" (qtd. in McClatchy, *Twenty Questions* 142). A renewal that does not replace the old but builds the new upon the foundation of the old (Berry 24). A renewal which becomes the epiphany of creation in the sacred texts of the *Kabbalah*:

> AN EPIPHANY enables you to sense creation not as something completed, but as constantly becoming, evolving, ascending. This transports you from a place where there is nothing new to a place where there is nothing old, where everything renews itself, where heaven and earth rejoice as at the moment of Creation. (Matt 99)

As J. D. McClatchy points out: "Not 'make it new,' but 'make it last' is their [contemporary poets'] motto" (*White Paper* 15). Contemporary poets seem primarily concerned with the superficialities of writing, such as career and publication, which only amount to seeking posterity (make it last): "No shortage, then, of honors, emoluments, publication possibilities, opportunities to garner public adulation. In such ways may contemporary poetry be said to be flourishing" (Epstein,

"Who Killed Poetry?" 15). Their true focus as writers, however, should be to uphold the tradition of poetic stewardship (make it new).

It is important to make this distinction: Poetic stewardship and posterity are not one in the same. Posterity seeks to accomplish the thing; stewardship exists in the process of creating the thing (Levertov 235). Posterity exists outside the poem; poetic stewardship exists completely within the poem. Posterity writes for an assumed tomorrow, which if it does not come, results in the total loss of the posterity; stewardship does not assume a tomorrow, but allows for it anyway within the moment of the present poem. Posterity exists solely to carry on the name of the poet; poetic stewardship exists solely to carry on the literary tradition. Stewardship is the inward assuming of all that is public—past, present and future.

In his book *The Poetry Wreck*, Karl Shapiro relates the legend of the "True Artificer," a legend that embodies the whole of stewardship:

> There is a legend about the end of the world which pictures a poet standing in the doorway of his lonely cottage, watching the approach of a pestilent cloud. He knows he is the last living man and he knows that death will come to him in a few hours. What does he do? How does he prepare for his own death and the death of the world? He does not sink down in thought or prayer; he does not attempt to record his final hours; he does not seek an escape from the inevitable destiny. He turns back into the house and goes to his writing table; he takes up the poem he is writing and studies it again. He begins the new corrections. (266–267)

CHAPTER SIX *poetic essence*

> Man only escapes from the laws of this world in lightning flashes. Instants when everything stands still, instants of contemplation, of pure intuition, of mental void, of acceptance of the moral void. It is through such instants that he is capable of the supernatural.
>
> —Simone Weil, *Gravity and Grace*

The function of poetry should be to "transfuse emotion—not to transmit thought but to set up in the reader's sense a vibration corresponding to what was felt by the writer[…]" (Housman 8). This essence, however, is being missed by most readers of contemporary American poetry, not only because the readers themselves have come to settle for less and are themselves numbed by the American culture of amusement, but also because the poets are not putting this essence into their poems. The essence is missing partly because the poets have retreated to the ramparts of academia, thus abandoning the battlefields of life and partly because there is a forgetting that poems need to be inextricably intertwined with life: "The interaction of life on art and of art on life is continuous. Poetry is necessary to a whole man, and that poetry be not divided from the rest of life is necessary to *it*. Both life and poetry fade, wilt, shrink, when they are divorced" (Levertov 134).

Denise Levertov sees poems as "testimonies of lived life, which is what writers have a vocation to give, and readers (including those who write) have a need to receive" (21). Paul Valéry states that, "Poetry is the very meeting point of mind and life—two indefinable essences" (3). The mass production of poetry has contributed greatly to corroding the connections between poetry and life. Bringing oneself into work everyday and thinking that one must produce a poem in order to keep one's teaching job, or produce a book in a certain amount of time, removes the life essence from the process of poetry. Writing becomes drudgery like mowing the lawn or taking out the trash. It no longer resonates on a deeper level to be written, but nags at a constant conscious level to be produced. As Randall Jarrell points out, "Everybody understands that poems and stories are written by memory and desire, love and hatred, daydreams and nightmares—by a being, not a brain" (89).

But contemporary poets have digressed from this fact in return for the comforts of living sheltered lives within academia. In fact, the MFA mills churn out poets so fast that students go straight into becoming teachers: "Many of these men and women go from being students in one writing program to being teachers in another—without, you might say, their feet, metrical or anatomical, having touched the floor" (Epstein, "Who Killed Poetry?" 14). Without this life experience, a lack of sincerity infects the poems, whereas, according to Tolstoy, it should be just the opposite: "Sincerity—is the most important of the three [conditions of the infection of art]. This condition is always present in popular art, which accounts for its powerful effect, and it is almost entirely absent in our upper-class art, ceaselessly fabricated by artists for reasons of personal gain or vanity" (122). Although Tolstoy was writing about another time and culture, the message rings true in contemporary American poetry. Bukowski reiterates:

> They are the piddlers in the field and most of the field are piddlers. These won't lay down any blood to get their work done, they won't gamble with madness, starvation in their need to get the work done. They don't feel it that way. They want fame and name but they won't give up their comforts and their securities. They just claim to be Artists and somehow feel that it will all come together for them. Meanwhile, they might live on hand-outs from relatives instead of having the guts to score for an ugly 8 hour job and try to break the walls from there. (199)

Ezra Pound states: "No artist can have too many experiences" (Essays 221). And Rainer Maria Rilke admonishes in his *Letters to a Young Poet*: "Write about what your everyday life offers you [...]" (7). Longinus, writing almost 1,800 years ago, said, "Inferior and average talent remains for the most part safe and faultless because it avoids risk and does not aim at the heights [...]" (45). Douglas Treem reminds us: "We literally look up to the 'high wire artist.' There is no such thing as a 'low wire artist.' And when the high wire artist tries to walk the low wire, it looks much like a drunk trying to 'walk the line'" ("Interview"). And as William Packard states: "You can't lead bunny lives and write tiger poetry" (Packard, "Editorial" 4).

It is exactly this scarce "trace of humanity" that leaves the poems lifeless, pointless and flat: "I hate these creampuff boys who've never lived badly enough or well enough or originally enough to have anything to write about" (Bukowski

183). This does not mean, however, that every poet must be a drunk or a psychotic or someone who has attempted suicide multiple times, as many poets today believe. This type of belief reflects the religious concept of not being able to be "saved" because one is not enough of a sinner—feeling that something is lacking in one's life because someone always gets up and gives a more reprehensible testimony of where they came from before joining the church. Poets today are depressed at how their ordinary lives pale in comparison to the "testimonials" of poets with messed up personal lives: "Innumerable young poets have drunk themselves into stupidity and cirrhosis because they admired John Berryman or Dylan Thomas and came to think they must drink like them to write like them. At the very least it is assumed that creativity and hang-ups are inevitably inseparable" (Levertov 187). It should also be pointed out that every drunk, crack whore or mental patient does not go on to become a great poet. Think of the many war poets; not everyone who goes to war becomes a poet, but when a poet goes to war he becomes a "war poet" (Treem).

It is not the circumstances, but the poets themselves, who make their circumstances mundane. Remember Rilke: "Write about what your everyday life offers you. If your everyday life seems poor, don't blame it; blame yourself" (7). While the first sentence has become a battle cry for contemporary poetry, it is the second sentence of this quotation that is most often forgotten. Poets, then, must have lives that are original for them and not follow in the footsteps of every Tom, Dick and Harry who has gotten an MFA. The fry cook can write interesting poetry, and more often than not, much more interesting poetry than the professor who has been locked away in the ivory tower. It is not because he is a fry cook, however; it is because he is more attuned to life itself than those existing within the academic vacuum. In speaking about what he calls the "legitimation crisis," Walter Kalaidjian states:

> This tension continues to be most deeply felt by academics, whose everyday professional lives deny the consoling models of community that humanism traditionally espouses. For better or for worse, most of our enduring verse writers are academics whose poetry typically seeks to repress and transcend their institutional lives. Often reproducing the professional regimen and bureaucratic functioning of the corporate world, academe has a hand in defining the writer's role, mixing its discourse little by little with poetry's lyric rhetoric. (26–27)

It is by removing the evidence of a lived life and by playing it safe, the poet evades the most important aspect of the poetic process: the inward going. Rainer Maria Rilke wrote in his *Letters to a Young Poet* some of the best writing advice ever given to a student of poetry:

> You ask me whether your verses are any good. You ask me. You have asked others before this. You send them to magazines. You compare them with other poems, and you are upset when certain editors reject your work. Now (since you have said you want my advice) I beg you to stop doing that sort of thing. You are looking outside, and that is what you should most avoid right now. No one can advise or help you—no one. There is only one thing you should do. Go into yourself. (5–6)

One of the three sayings inscribed above the entrance to the Oracle of Delphi is a simple command: "γνῶθι σεαυτὸν" (gnothi seauton, know thyself). As Charles Bukowski wrote to William Packard: "The human and the word cannot be separated" (67). It is the greatest risk of all to go within one's own psyche and explore its depths and voids. It is an even greater risk to summon inner daemons and expose them and explore their relationship to the outside world: "What poetry most significantly celebrates is the capacity of man to face the deep, dark inwardness of his nature and his fate" (Warren 31). As Rilke continues, "And it is out of this turning—within, out of this immersion in your own world, poems come, then you will not think of asking whether they are good or not" (8–9).

The poem should be the record of this inward journey. The journey into one's own soul. C. K. Williams says, "The poem is the most direct means of communication with the soul" (28):

> I suppose that I do think of poetry as, if not a passion of the soul, then the voice of the passion of the soul [...]. Even a nourishment of the soul, and indeed of society, in that it keeps alive the sense of self and the correlated sense of a community.
>
> Poetry even, in the same act and the same moment, helps one to grasp reality and to grasp one's own life. Not that it will give definitions and certainties. But it can help us to ponder on what St. Augustine meant when he said that he was a question to himself. (Warren 92)

Once we have been to the soul and contemplated that

within us, the soul turns into pure desire for all that is beautiful:

> This thirst belongs to the immortality of Man. It is at once a consequence and an indication of his perennial existence. It is the desire of the moth for the star. It is no mere appreciation of the beauty before us—but a wild effort to reach the beauty above. (Poe 77)

sublimation of being

Dry ice (frozen carbon dioxide) exemplifies the scientific principle of sublimation. Transforming from a solid state directly to an ethereal, gaseous state filling the surrounding area with clouds of "smoke," dry ice is "dry" because it passes from a solid to a gas without ever becoming a liquid. Mothballs also demonstrate the scientific principle of sublimation. The white crystalline chemical naphthalene, which makes up mothballs, vaporizes directly from a solid to a gas, permeating the surrounding space with a familiar yet pungent smell. Sublimation, then, can be viewed as the emanation of a substance's essence from the tangible to the ethereal.

The Greek word for sublime, hypsos (ὕψος), literally means "to rise to some height." The English word is derived from the Latin *sub* meaning "up to" and *limen* meaning "lintel" ("Sublime"). This rising to a great height, or to almost any height above the head, as in the door's lintel, is itself a metaphor for a passage to knowledge and understanding. The term is used in a scientific manner by Sigmund Freud to describe the appearance of unconscious thought in conscious actions, a "sublimation" of thought processes that resemble the creative process ("Sublimation").

Longinus wrote about the results of the creative process over a century and a half earlier in his famous book *On the Sublime* (Περὶ Ὕψους). In this essay, Longinus addresses Postumius Terentianus as a rebuttal to the supposedly inaccurate rendering of the sublime by the writer Caecilius. Longinus uses the sublime as a way to explain the reaction a reader may have to a great work:

> Any piece of writing which is heard repeatedly by a man of intelligence and experience yet fails to stir his soul to noble thoughts and does not leave impressed upon his mind reflections which reach beyond what was said, and which on further observation is seen to fade and be forgotten—that is not truly great writing, as it is only remembered while it is before us. The truly great can be pondered again and again; it is difficult, indeed impossible to withstand, for the memory of it is strong and hard to efface. (10)

In addressing Longinus' work, George Saintsbury proposes that this Longinian sublimity has its origins in the creative process itself:

> In endeavoring to provide something more satisfactory, especially as to the sources of Sublimity, he premises little more in the shape of definition than that it is "a certain consummateness and eminence" of words, completing this with the remark (the first epoch-making one of the trea-

tise) that the effect of such things is 'not persuasion but transport,' not the result of skill, pains and arrangement, but something which, "opportunely out-flung," carries everything before it. (1: 155)

Longinus attributes this sublime process to the imitation of the classics by comparing the reading and studying of the classics to the Priestess of Delphi inhaling divine vapors that allowed her to utter oracles (22).

The concept of imitation, however, is more complex than just the study of classics. Aristotle proposed that one origin of poetry was in imitation: "Imitation is natural to man from childhood, one of his advantages over the lower animals being this, that he is the most imitative creature in the world, and learns at first by imitation. And it is also natural for all to delight in works of imitation" (Aristotle 1457). The nature imitated can be viewed as both arising out of an inward nature, as well as an outward nature. It is this inward nature that is sublimated from the unconscious to the conscious in Freudian theory.[13] Viewing this imitation as a mirror of sorts, it can be seen, as Hegel saw, that "any mention of Essence implies that we distinguish it from Being: [...] The point of view given by the Essence is in general the standpoint of 'Reflection' " (Hegel 130). Therefore, the solid (being) emits a vapor (imitation/reflection/essence) via sublimation. If the essence is a reflection of being, then the true imitation is more likely to be that of the inner self than that of the facade of mankind and society. Thus when a poem or piece of prose resonates with one's inner self, this dynamic between essence and be-

---

13   It could also be said that the outward nature is sublimated from the unconscious to the conscious through contemplation.

ing is established, bringing about a deeper and more revered understanding of the work. It is precisely this resonance brought about through sublimation that creates the passion Longinus addresses in his treatise: "For I would make bold to say that nothing contributes to greatness as much as noble passion in the right place; it breathes the frenzied spirit of its inspiration upon the words and makes them, as it were, prophetic" (11). Ezra Pound uses this "charging" of the words in his definition of great literature: "Great Literature is simply language charged with meaning to the utmost possible degree" (*Essays* 23). This "charging" implies that the author imparts a potential energy into the language that will be released through the process of sublimation.

It was Immanuel Kant's concept of the innate sublimity of man himself, which also helped call the attention of the sublime to the Romantics: "Man's dignity is the ground of the judgement that man himself is sublime" (Goldthwait 25).

The agreement of the two above hypotheses is seen in both Shelley and Wordsworth. Shelley describes poetry as "'the expression of the imagination': and poetry is connate with the origin of man" (480). Wordsworth writes:

> Poetry is the image of man and nature. [...] The Poet writes under one restriction only, namely, the necessity of giving immediate pleasure to a human Being possessed of that information which may be expected from him, not as a lawyer, a physician, a mariner, an astronomer, or a natural philosopher, but as a Man. (938)

In both cases, the author is using Kantian sublimity to define poetry.

Wordsworth continues by saying: "Poetry is the breath and finer spirit of all knowledge; it is the impassioned expression which is in the countenance of all science" (938). Paul Valéry expands upon the metaphor of poetry being the breath of knowledge by claiming, "Thought is, in short, the activity which causes what does not exist to come alive in us, lending to it, whether we will or no, our present powers, making us take the part for the whole, the image for reality [...]" (73). J. D. McClatchy extends this theme by saying: "Sublime is a tone, but a tone raised to such a pitch that it becomes subject matter, and a subject at the height of poetic ambition" (*Twenty Questions* 147). Valéry completes the metaphor of the sublime by asserting, "It is the poet's business to give us the feeling of an intimate union between the word and the mind" (74).

Poetry becomes sublime through the convergence of both word and mind, this breath of knowledge. When words rise to this lofty area of thought and understanding, one feels the barbaric yawp of Whitman. Just like the "smoke" from the dry ice and the permeating aroma from the mothballs, language charged with meaning billows toward the top of the doorframe by emanating an understanding that can only be conveyed through a resonance with one's innermost being. The poetic sublime, then, is the etherization of the poet's essence through language.

CHAPTER SEVEN *myth*

For poetry ultimately has to do most of all with that, with the redemption of our experiences from the temporal and trivial.

—C. K. Williams, *Poetry and Consciousness*

Contemporary American poetry lacks the etherization of essence by lacking the mythological, poetry filled with meaningless details about Grandma so-and-so, their dog, Spot, or other arcane and irrelevant details, which flood the sense out of most contemporary poems. These poems fail to utilize details for what they are intended: The creation of the mythological. Instead of making the ordinary, extraordinary, as in the mythological, they make the ordinary even more mundane.

In her essay "Against Decoration," Mary Karr lists the overuse of meaningless references as a form of obscurity (59). Denise Levertov warns that one should not necessarily be able to extract a biography from the poetry (175). And Christopher Clausen states:

Today the reflection of reality in poetry has come for many poets to mean the documentation of often meaningless details—frequently details of the poet's inner life. [...] This view of reality has led to a poetic context that is at the same time both trivial and presumptuous. (125)

As Christopher Clausen points out, it was William Wordsworth who first opened the door, at least in more modern times, to the introduction of personal elements into poetry when he listed "the recollection of childhood" as a sixth human experience eligible to be written about in poetry (124).[14] First, Walt Whitman, then Ezra Pound would perfect this use; its climax coming in the 1960s with the Confessional poets. Whitman and Pound have always contained a certain mythological quality to their work, a quality that incorporates both specific historical and personal references. What, then, sets these poets apart from the demise of contemporary American Poetry?

Denise Levertov suggests:

> All that is most interesting about an artist's life must be in the work itself. There the autobiographical is often completely transformed, or, if undisguisedly recounted, is selected, and invested with a significance which transcends the ephemeral and narrowly personal. When this transcendence does not take place, autobiographical material lacks the resonance we find in poems pervaded by a larger context. (174)

Levertov continues to explain: "Yeats' Maude Gonne is not just Maude Gonne, and the poet is not just Willy Yeats who was in love with her. She is Cathleen Ni Houlihan, she is Ireland herself, and the Irish people in love with their country" (174). As to Milosz, she writes: "[He] only writes explicitly

---

14 Wordsworth's five other human experiences: Love, Death, War, Religion, and external Nature.

of his own life-story as much as is demanded by his major theme, the human intellect and the human soul within the turmoil of twentieth century history" (174–175). And of William Carlos Williams, whom she acknowledges as strongly emphasizing the concrete image, she writes: "No one could extract a biography from his *Collected Poems*" (175). The same holds true for both Whitman and Pound. Whitman did not include personal references for the sake of autobiography, but as a biographical element to the greater persona of America itself; a grounding of the greater persona in the personal experience. It *is* possible to read Whitman and not know that he was a homosexual, he had a severely dysfunctional family, or many other irrelevant details to the Whitman that is related to us as America. Graham Clarke says of Whitman: "Whitman, like his message, remains ambiguous and diffident. The actual Whitman 'hides' within the ideal Whitman" (26). Pound is even more complex in the sense that his persona, *Ego Scriptor*, makes reference to the history of the entire world. Christopher Clausen points to Pound's development as moving away from the poem-as-object, and "toward the poem as didactic myth" (90). Clarke sums up this issue when he speaks of Whitman: "The poetry is the site of that dialectic: a private history which hovers beneath the public projection of individual and cultural myth" (26).

Both Pound and Whitman were keenly aware of the historicity surrounding what they were doing. Their references were such that historical details may be recalled by both poet and reader; no matter how difficult the references were to understand, they were at least accessible on some level. Many contemporary poets, however, use personal references which have no meaning to the reader—references which have no meaning to the reader without the reader knowing every detail of the poet's life.

Specific, personal references do not mean the type of references that Whitman or Pound included in their poetry, such as specific place names, historical people, historical facts. All of these references are traceable, even mean something when taken into the general context of the poem without specifically knowing who or what they are. Contemporary poets, however, make reference to Aunt Sally, their friend Billy, Bo or Bob, their dog, their child, their gardener, etc., and build a poem around that simple understanding.

It is important to remember at this point that poetry is inherently cyclical in nature—meaning that it is meant to be read over and over again—and with each new reading a greater depth of understanding is met (Wordsworth 941). With the use of specific details and references, it is important that a *subjective understanding* take place on the first reading. The reference, whether or not that reference is completely known to the reader, becomes immediately recognized. Then, when the reader remembers or researches the particular reference, he or she reaches an *objective understanding*, upon subsequent readings. At this point, most contemporary poets fail.[15] Often there is a subjective understanding of a reference; it is obvious on the first reading that this reference belongs. But if the reader does not fully understand who Grandma Sally is or no further connection is made to

---

15 Many contemporary poems fail at the subjective understanding level with misplaced or non-existent modifiers, assuming that the reader will figure out the pronominal referent; however, if this referent is unclear on the first reading, then the poem also falls flat and never transcends to an objective understanding.

Grandma Sally, there is never an objective understanding of the overall relevance of the poem. This leaves the poem flat and the reader wondering just who Grandma Sally was, is, or worse, simply not wondering about her at all. Once again the prosaism of contemporary poetry is obvious. Without the ability to discover an objective understanding of the poem on subsequent readings, the poem needs only to be read once, just like prose.

The majority of references used today in poems, though, exist within the poem not because of a reach for the mythological, but as an emulation of the Confessional poets. It was with the Confessional poets the use of personal details reached its zenith of understanding. In many poems today, the inclusion of those details is poorly performed and confusing. Critics once questioned this practice when the Confessional poets first came to the forefront. Writing about Robert Lowell's *Life Studies*, Robert Bly states: "In this country's poems the facts are put in because they happened, regardless of how much they lame the poem" (27). Denise Levertov, however, defends Lowell on the grounds of his craftsmanship, stating that his philosophy is different, originally, but now distorted with time. In other words, Lowell still had enough skill to pull off the details in his poems, "By his overriding historical sense, which places all that stems from his individual history into a larger objective configuration" (Levertov 177). As more and more contemporary poets simply try to copy what the Confessionals were doing, the "Xerox syndrome"[16] occurs again. Without the historical understanding surrounding it, the emulation has watered down

---

16   See Chapter 3 for a complete discussion of the "Xerox syndrome."

the use of personal details to the point of boring gibberish: "As an ideal, it seemed particularly congenial to democratic and visionary poets, though in lesser hands than Blake's and Whitman's the visionary contemplation of common particulars has often degenerated into the tedious notation of all life's trivia" (Clausen 18).

However, Ezra Pound admonishes: "Go in fear of abstractions" (*Essays* 5). So the balance of specifics against the fear of abstractions becomes the razor's edge of the mythological. William Packard suggests that proper nouns should be used as frequently as possible to enter both the sound and the sense of the poem. Proper nouns will, at times, provide interesting sounds within the poem that can be expanded upon or worked with in the context of the poem. In other words: "Craft can open up intuition" (Packard, "Craft Lecture"). The utilization of these specifics also allows the poet to go much deeper into the sense or meaning of the poem. Using nothing but generalities allows the poet to hide behind non-specifics and create what Packard calls "peek-a-boo" poems—poems that allow the reader only a hint of what is actually going on, and, more importantly, hide the true meaning of the poem from the poets themselves ("Craft Lecture"). Robert Bly says, "Abstraction is merely another form of the flight from inwardness; the objectivist takes flight into the outward world, and the rationalist into the efficient intellect" (30). Put another way: "Generality is necessary to the advancement of knowledge; but particularity is indispensable to the creations of the imagination" (Lord Macaulay qtd. in Clausen 15). The skill in the use of specifics comes to play once the true meaning of the poem has been established. The specifics may fit right into the poem and demand to stay, or they may no longer serve a purpose and may be removed. If the specifics stay within the poem, they must somehow make the leap from private to public as Vernon Shetley observes: "The Project of creating an autobiographical myth itself implies [...] translation of private experience into public terms [...]" (75). The making of the ordinary into the extraordinary.

It is the transubstantiation of this inwardness to the public venue that is the key to separating mundane facts from a personal mythology. As Wendell Berry puts it: "[Poetry] is a seeking of self in words [...]" (14). Robert Penn Warren reminds us that this self intertwined with the greater mythos extends back to the time of the Greeks:

> When the Greeks hit upon the notion of man as the measure of all things, they hit, as a corollary, upon the notion of the self as the central fact of "poetry." The notion was, in its manifestations, aristocratic, even heroic. Gods and goddesses, kings and queens, heroes and heroines populate the narrative of Homer, but we recognize them now as human "selves" of great variety and depth. (xiv)

Stanley Plumly uses Charles Wright as an example:

> Wright's book of epiphanies, his book of emblems, his book of lines, manifests a fundamental tension between the "triviality" of the local object and its will for "transubstantiation," between the body and will of the poet. [...] The ambition of any emblem is to speak of things beyond their occasion and keep watch of things immense and unspeakable. And the ideas of ideas is that there be such a thing as meaning outside the corporation of the body, a

meaning beyond memory. (II, 32)

And as J. D. McClatchy observes about myth: "If by myth we mean not just stories of gods and beasts but gods and beasts as metaphors of the inner life, powers that control or liberate us, that help us make sense of the world—or, in Merwin's own formulation, 'intuitions of a kind of coherent sense of experience, which we can't live without'" (*Twenty Questions* 141). Obviously through Merwin's embedded quotation, one can see that the characters or events do not have to be "mythological" in the sense of Sir James Frazier, or Joseph Campbell-type myth, but a personal mythos that is created out of the inward life and projected, albeit understandably, into the public domain:

> And therefore it is the prime merit of genius, and its most unequivocal mode of manifestations so to represent familiar objects as to awaken in the minds of others a kindred feeling concerning them, and that freshness of sensation which is the constant accompaniment of menial no less than of bodily convalescence. (Coleridge 49)

In other words, if the entire poem requires us to know Grandma Sally, and we don't learn what we need to know about her in the poem itself and can not eventually take that relationship and apply it to our own historical knowledge of our own grandmothers, then the poem will fall flat.

Roland Barthes makes the connection between myth and history unmistakable: "It [the very principle of myth] transforms history into nature" (129). The connection is even more poignant when seen as a negative: "And the mythless man remains externally hungering amid the past, and digs and grubs for roots [...]" (Nietzsche 85).

Barthes suggests: "Myth lends itself to history in two ways; by its form, which is only relatively motivated; by its concept, the nature of which is historical" (137). Myth must be grounded in an historical reality in order to be understood: "What the world supplies to myth is a historical reality, defined, even if this goes back quite a while, by the way in which men have produced or used it; and what myth gives in return is a *natural* image of this reality" (Barthes 142). It is only through this grounding in history that myth can be understood within a poem. Roland Barthes sees the language of mythology as being a metalanguage; herein lies the irony. While mythological language falls in line with Postmodern theory by being a "metalanguage," Postmodernism, itself, undermines that level of language by removing the historical references from the scaffolding which is required to support the myth's metalanguage:

> It can be seen that in myth there are two semiological systems, one of which is staggered in relation to the other: a linguistic system, the language (or the modes of representation which are assimilated to it), which I shall call the *language-object*, because it is the language which myth gets hold of in order to build its own system; and myth itself, which I shall call *metalanguage*, because it is a second language, *in which* one speaks about the first. (Barthes 115)

By Barthes transcending myth from language to a metalanguage, he has added to its importance and has created problems for the poet. Myth, then, cannot simply be understood in terms of the language itself within a poem, but relies more heavily on that language to import enough meaning to support the metalanguage of the myth. This adds to the importance of the already crucial language used in the poem.

The poet, then, creates the myth out of language. The myth is not formed by words alone but is formed by all that is said surrounding the words:

> Our best poets continue to see the grain of sand alight with eternity, continue to attend to the grit of the first things and to the magnitude of the last, and to how both crisscross and constitute the daily life.[...] Our important poets use the fictions of autobiography or the logic of dreams, the grammar of history or the hermetic codes of memory—any and all of these, images and ideas, to make poems that both matter and enspirit, challenge and console. (McClatchy, *White Paper* 13)

As Rilke reminds us: "Trust in things [...] in the small things that hardly anyone sees and that can so suddenly become huge, immeasurable" (Rilke 33). Create myth. Make the ordinary, extraordinary.

CONCLUSION

Poetry is not dead. Only the idea of what poetry should be is dead.

—Charles Bukowski, *Reach for the Sun*

And yet, Karl Shapiro, Dana Gioia, Edmund Wilson and others who prophesy the death of poetry are wrong. Poets have simply allowed poetry's once bright flames to be smothered by the bell jar of amusement, creating the appearance of an amplified flame while simultaneously depriving the flickering flames of precious oxygen. This oxygen can only be breathed back into poetry from the souls of the poets themselves, by allowing the Muse to regain a prominent place in both thinking and theory.

Amusement has given society the freedom not to think or push themselves in any inward pursuits. Buying into the dance of a stripper at the Paradise Club or Mickey Mouse on Main Street USA, the phony smile forced on their plastic faces tells all: "Give me money and I will provide you with unsubstantiated fantasy." Shadow becomes substance.

As Doug Treem once said, "It's like using McDonald's to rid the world of hunger" ("Interview"). One cannot cure society's ills by force feeding them food which lacks substance. Rather we hear Kenneth Patchen's admonishment: "The one who comes to question himself has cared for mankind." Poets must search within themselves in order to tap into the Muse and allow it to flourish in their lives and more importantly in the life of their poetry.

Despite the fact that the MFA programs have demystified poetry by removing the Muse, schools need to realize that the Muse can be taught in a circumambient fashion. First, there is no need to rush to become a poet. There is a greater need for poets to have experienced life, than to be cranked out of an MFA program and deemed a "poet" in only two years. Second, poets can be taught how to feed their Muse nutritional material by teaching them a literary stewardship and instilling a tradition which exists through them emanating from the past and toward a future. This tradition should be in lieu of the current emphasis on the rush for posterity, being published in order to complete school, getting teaching jobs, and then keeping those jobs. There is also a need for each poet to develop his or her own voice along the way by emphasizing the Muse and stewardship equally with craft. By only reading their teachers and other contemporary poets, the students have already limited their knowledge to that of, at best, a copy of a copy of a technique. By reading across time and cultures and "reading what the Masters read," as Basho would say (qtd. by Treem, "Interview"), poets can develop their own voice and avoid the "Xerox syndrome."

There is nothing wrong with the fact that so many people today want to become poets. The astonishing rise in poetry's popularity can only be viewed as an overall good thing. However, when the system that greets these potential poets fails to provide one half of the instruction needed to become a poet, the future poets themselves are already doomed in

their education. Academia is a surreal world of financial security, and the trade off for that security is the push to produce on demand, to teach only the tangible craft of poetry.
But neither of these exclusive techniques provide any room
for a burgeoning Muse to properly develop.

If the bell jar were to be shattered, allowing the Muses
to breathe, the flame could again burn brightly, and it is
through this uninhibited flame that poets should be fever-
ishly signaling.

Adler, Mortimer J. Poetry and Politics. Pittsburgh, PA: Duquesne UP, 1965.

Altieri, Charles. Self and Sensibility in Contemporary American Poetry. Cambridge Studies in American Literature and Culture, Ed. Albert Gelpi. Cambridge: Cambridge UP, 1984.

Aristotle. The Basic Works of Aristotle. Trans. Richard McKeon. New York: Random House, 1941.

Arnold, Matthew. Essays in Criticism. Boston: Ticknor and Fields, 1865.

Artaud, Antonin. The Theater and Its Double (Le Théâtre et son Double). 1938. Trans. Mary Caroline Richards. New York: Grove Press, 1958.

Atwood, Margaret. "Poetic Process?" A Field guide to Contemporary Poetry and Poetics. Eds. Stuart Friebert and David Young. New York: Logman, 1980.

Barthes, Roland. Mythologies. (1957) Trans. Annette Lavers. (1972) New York: Hill and Wang, 1972.

Beach, Christopher. "Careers in Creativity: The Poetry Academy in the 1990's." Western Humanities Review. 50:1, Spring 1996, 4–16.

Bentham, Jeremy. The Works of Jeremy Bentham. Reproduction of the Bowring Ed. of 1838-1843. New York: Russell and Russell, Inc., 1962. (I:539-541, 583; II: 212-213, 252-254).

Bernstein, Charles. <u>A Poetics</u>. Cambridge: Harvard UP, 1992.

- - -. <u>Contents Dream: Essays 1975 – 1984</u>. Los Angeles: Sun and Moon Press, 1986.

Berry, Wendell. "The Specialization of Poetry." 1975. <u>The Poet's Work: 29 Masters of Twentieth Century Poetry on the Origins and Practice of their Art</u>. Ed. Reginald Gibbons. Boston: Houghton Mifflin Co., 1979. 139–56.

Black, Stephen A. <u>Whitman's Journeys into Chaos: A Psychoanalytic Study of the Poetic Process</u>. Princeton: Princeton UP, 1975.

Bloom, Harold. <u>The Anxiety of Influence: A Theory of Poetry</u>. 2nd ed. New York: Oxford U P, 1997.

Bly, Robert. <u>American Poetry: Wildness and Domesticity</u>. New York: Harper and Row, Publishers, 1990.

Breslin, James E. B. <u>From Modern to Contemporary: American Poetry, 1945-1965</u>. Chicago: The U of Chicago P, 1984.

Breton, André. <u>Manifestoes of Surrealism</u>. Trans. Richard Seaver and Helen R. Lane. Ann Arbor: U of Michigan P, 1969.

Bukowski, Charles. <u>Reach for the Sun: Selected Letters 1978 – 1994, Volume 3</u>. Ed. Seamus Cooney. Santa Rosa: Black Sparrow Press, 1999.

Carlyle, Thomas. <u>On Heroes, Hero-Worship and the Heroic in History</u>. 1840. Reprint of the 1897 ed. London: Chapman and Hall. New York: AMS Press, 1980.

Carruth, Hayden. "Poetry and Academicism." <u>Sewanee Review</u> 94 (1986): 335–336.

Cassill, R. V. "Comments." AWP Convention. Boston. 1982. (Unpublished speech).

Clarke, Graham. <u>Walt Whitman: The Poem as Private History</u>. New York: St. Martin's Press, 1991.

Clausen, Christopher. The Place of Poetry: Two Centuries of an Art in Crisis. Lexington, KY: UP of Kentucky, 1981.

Coleridge, Samuel Taylor. Biographia Literaria: or Biographical Sketches of My Literary Life and Opinions. 1817. Everyman's Library Edition. Ed. George Watson. London: J. M. Dent & Sons Ltd.; Rutland, VT: Charles E. Tuttle Co., Inc., 1991.

Collins, Christopher. Lecture. New York University, New York. 22 October 1996.

- - -. The Poetics of the Mind's Eye: Literature and the Psychology of Imagination. Philadelphia: U of Pennsylvania P, 1991.

Dante. De Vulgari Eloquentia. Trans. Steven Botterill. Cambridge Medieval Classics 5. Ed. Peter Dronke. Cambridge: Cambridge UP, 1996.

Dickey, James. "Craft Interview With James Dickey." The New York Quarterly 10 (1972): 16–35.

Disch, Thomas M. The Castle of Indolence: On Poetry, Poets and Poetasters. New York: Picador, 1995.

Eliot, T. S. The Complete Poems and Plays: 1909-1950. New York: Harcourt Brace & Company, 1980.

- - -. Selected Prose of T. S. Eliot. Ed. Frank Kermode. New York: Harcourt Brace Jovanovich, Farrar, Strauss and Giroux, 1975.

Epstein, Joseph. "What to do About the Arts." Commentary Apr. 1995: 23-30.

- - -. "Who Killed Poetry?" Commentary Aug. 1988: 13–20.

Frederick, John T. "The Place of Creative Writing in American Schools." English Journal 22 (1933): 8–16.

Fredman, Stephen. Poet's Prose: The Crisis in American Verse. 1983. 2nd Ed. Cambridge: Cambridge UP, 1990.

Freedman, Morris. "How Dead is Poetry?" The Virginia Quarterly Review 71 (1995): 315–320.

Forrest-Thompson, Veronica. Poetic Artifice: A Theory of Twentieth-century Poetry. New York: St. Martin's Press, 1978.

Frost, Robert. "Between Prose and Verse." The Atlantic Monthly January 1962: 51–54.

Garrett, George. "The Future of Creative Writing Programs." Creative Writing in America. Ed. Joseph M. Moxley. Urbana, Illinois: National Council of Teachers of English, 1989. 47–61.

Gioia, Dana. Can Poetry Matter? Essays on Poetry and American Culture. Saint Paul: Graywolf Press, 1992.

Goldthwait, John T. Introduction. Observations on the Feeling of the Beautiful and Sublime. By Immanuel Kant. Trans. John T. Goldthwait. 1960. Berkeley: U of California P, 1991.

Grimes, Tom. "The Workshop's Evolution and the Writer's Life." The Writer's Chronicle September 1999: 19–30.

Gummere, Francis B. Democracy and Poetry. Northwestern University: The N. W. Harris Lectures for 1911. Boston: Houghton Mifflin Co., 1911.

Haines, John. "Further Reflections on Line and the Poetic Voice." A Field Guide to Contemporary Poetry. Ed. Stuart Friebert and David Young. New York: Longman, 1989. 69–73.

Hall, Donald. Death to the Death of Poetry: Essays, Reviews, Notes, Interviews. Poets on Poetry. Ann Arbor: The U of Michigan P, 1997.

- - -. "The Line." In A Field Guide to Contemporary Poetry. Ed. Stuart Friebert and David Young. New York: Longman, 1989. 73–75.

- - -. "Poetry and Ambition." What is a Poet? Essays from the Eleventh Alabama Symposium on English and American Literature. Ed. Hank Lazer. Tuscaloosa: U of Alabama P, 1987. 229–246.

Heaney, Seamus. The Redress of Poetry. New York: Farrar, Straus and Giroux, 1995.

Hegel. "The Doctrine of Essence." Hegel Selections. 1929. Trans. W. Wallace. Ed. Jacob Loewenberg. New York: Charles Scribner's Sons, 1957. 129–217.

Hesiod. Hesiod: The Works and Days, Theogony, The Shield of Herakles. Trans. Richard Lattimore. 1959. Ann Arbor: U of Michigan P, 1991.

Hirshfield, Jane. "The Question of Originality." The American Poetry Review July/August 1989: 7–13.

Holden, Jonathan. The Fate of American Poetry. Athens: U of Georgia P, 1991.

- - -. The Rhetoric of the Contemporary Lyric. Bloomington: Indiana UP, 1980.

- - -. Style and Authenticity in Postmodern Poetry. Columbia: U of Missouri P, 1986.

Hollander, John. The Work of Poetry. New York: Columbia UP, 1997.

Hollis, Karyn. "Nicaraguan Poetry Workshops: The Democratization of Poetry." Studies in Latin American Popular Culture 11 (1992): 109–122.

Holub, Robert C. Reception Theory: A Critical Introduction. New York: Methuen, 1984.

Horace (Quintus Horatius Flaccus). "Ars Poetica." Horace: Satires and Epistles; Persius: Satires. Trans. Niall Rudd. London: Penguin Books, 1979. 190–203.

Housman, A. E. The Name and Nature of Poetry. New York: The MacMillan Company, 1933.

Howard, Richard. Alone with America: Essays on the Art of Poetry in the United States since 1950. New York: Athenum, 1969.

"ὕψος" (Hypsos). An Intermediate Greek–English Lexicon: Founded Upon The Seventh Edition of Liddell and Scott's Greek–English Lexicon. 1886. Oxford: The Clarendon Press, 1996.

Jarrell, Randall. Poetry and the Age. New York: Alfred A. Knopf, 1953.

Kalaidjian, Walter. Languages of Liberation: The Social Text in Contemporary American Poetry. New York: Columbia UP, 1989.

Karr, Mary. "Against Decoration." Viper Rum. New York: New Directions Press, 1998.

Kinzie, Mary. The Cure of Poetry in an Age of Prose: Moral Essays on the Poet's Calling. Chicago: The U of Chicago P, 1993.

"Kubla Khan." The Oxford Companion to English Literature. 5th ed. 1985.

Kunert, Günter. "Why Write?" 1972. Trans. James Hulbert. The Poet's Work: 29 Masters of Twentieth Century Poetry on the Origins and Practice of Their Art. Ed. Reginal Gibbons. Boston: Houghton Mifflin Co., 1979. 136–138.

Kuzma, Greg. "The Catastrophe of Creative Writing." Poetry September 1986: 342–354.

Lazer, Hank. "Critical Theory and Contemporary American Poetry." What is a Poet? Essays from the Eleventh Alabama Symposium on English and American Literature. Ed. Hank Lazer. Tuscaloosa: U of Alabama P, 1987.

- - -. Opposing Poetries: Volume One: Issues and Institutions. Vol. 1. Evanston: Northwestern UP, 1996.

Lea, Sydney. "Democracy and the Demotic: Reflections on the 'Lingua Franca et Jocundissima' in American Poetry." New England Review Summer 1994: 11–18.

Levertov, Denise. New and Selected Essays. New York: New Directions Press, 1992.

Longinus. On Great Writing (On the Sublime). Trans. G. M. A. Grube. Indianapolis: Hackett Publishing Company, Inc., 1991.

Lowell, Amy. Poetry and Poets: Essays. 1930. New York: Biblo and Tannen, 1971.

Matt, Daniel C. The Essential Kabbalah: The Heart of Jewish Mysticism. 1995. Edison, New Jersey: Castle Books, 1997.

Matthews, William. "A Note on Prose, Verse, and the Line." <u>A Field Guide to Contemporary Poetry</u>. Ed. Stuart Friebert and David Young. New York: Longman, 1989. 77–78.

McClatchy, J. D. <u>Twenty Questions.</u> New York: Columbia UP, 1998.

- - -. <u>White Paper: On Contemporary American Poetry</u>. New York: Columbia UP, 1989.

McNair, Wesley. "On Poets, Poets Teaching, and Poetry: Notes from a Journal." <u>Ploughshares</u> 24 (1998): 146–156.

McPherson, Sandra. "The Working Line." <u>A Field Guide to Contemporary Poetry</u>. Ed. Stuart Friebert and David Young. New York: Longman, 1989. 57–64.

Metzidakis, Stamos. "Breton and Poetic Originality." <u>André Breton Today</u>. Ed. Anna Balakian and Rudolf E. Kuenzli. New York: Willis Locker and Owens, 1989. 28–35.

Mill, John Stuart. "Thoughts on Poetry and Its Varieties." 1833. <u>Autobiography and Literary Essays</u>. Ed. John M. Robson and Jack Stillinger. Routledge: U of Toronto P, 1981.

Miller, James E., Jr. <u>Leaves of Grass: America's Lyric-Epic of Self and Democracy</u>. New York: Twayne Publishers, 1992.

Moore, Todd. "The Present State of American Poetry." <u>The New York Quarterly</u> 57 (1997): 108–116.

Muir, Edwin. <u>The Estate of Poetry</u>. St. Paul: Graywolf Press, 1993.

"Muse." <u>Oxford English Dictionary</u>. 2nd ed. 1989.

"Muses." <u>The Oxford Classical Dictionary</u>. 3rd ed. 1996.

Myers, David Gershom. <u>Educating Writers: The Beginnings of "Creative Writing" in the American University</u>. Diss. Northwestern U, 1989. Ann Arbor: UMI, 1999.

Nietzsche, Friedrich. <u>The Birth of Tragedy</u>. (1872). Trans. Clifton P. Fadiman. New York: Dover Publications, Inc., 1995.

Olson, Charles. "Projective Verse." 1950. <u>Poetics of the New American Poetry</u>. Ed. Donald Allen and Warren Tallman. New York:

Grove Press, 1973. 147–158.

Packard, William. Craft Lecture. Contemporary American Poetry Workshop. New York University, New York. 23 September 1999.

- - -. Editorial. The NewYork Quarterly 45 (1991): 3–14.

- - -. Personal interview. 2 February 1999.

Patchen, Kenneth. "The One Who Comes." Internet. Http://www. ourworld.compuserve.com/homepages/Patchen/patcal.htm. February, 1996.

Peacock, Thomas Love. The Works of Thomas Love Peacock. 1820. Vol. 3. London: Richard Bentley and Son, 1875.

Perry, Marion J. H. Master of Fine Arts Programs: The Training of Professional Writers as Artists. Diss. State University of New York at Buffalo, 1985. Ann Arbor: UMI, 1999.

Pinsky, Robert. "American Poetry in American Life." American Poetry Review March/April 1996: 19–23.

- - -. "Responsibilities of the Poet." Craft Lecture at the Napa Poetry Conference, August 1984. Politics & Poetic Value. Ed. Robert von Hallberg. Chicago: The U of Chicago P, 1987.

- - -. The Situation of Poetry: Contemporary Poetry and It's Traditions. Princeton: Princeton UP, 1976.

Plato. The Dialogues of Plato. Trans. B. Jowett. 2 vols. New York: Random House, 1937.

Plumly, Stanley. "Chapter and Verse." 2 Pt. Series. American Poetry Review Jan./Feb. and May/June 1978: 21–32.

Poe, Edgar Allan. Essays and Reviews. New York: The Library of America, 1984.

Pound, Ezra. ABC of Reading. 1934. New York: New Directions Press, n.d.

- - -. The Cantos of Ezra Pound. New York: New Directions, 1989.

- - -. Literary Essays of Ezra Pound. Ed. T. S. Eliot. New York: New

Directions Press, 1918.

"Practice and Profession of the Arts: Preparation of the Artist: Academies and the Artistic Elite." <u>Encyclopaedia Britannica</u>. CD-ROM. 1998.

Reeve, F. D. "What's the Matter with Poetry?" <u>The Nation</u> 24 May 1993: 708–712.

Rilke, Rainer Maria. <u>Letters to a Young Poet.</u> Trans. Stephen Mitchell. New York: Vintage Books, 1984.

Ryan, Judith. "Dead Poet's Voices: Rilke's 'Lost from the Outset' and the Originality Effect." <u>Modern Language Quaterly</u> 53.2 (1992): 227–246.

Saintsbury, George. <u>A History of Criticism and Literary Taste in Europe from the Earliest Texts to the Present Day</u>. 3 vols. Edinburgh: William Blackwood and Sons Ltd., 1949.

Schwartz, Delmore. <u>Selected Essays of Delmore Schwartz</u>. Ed. Donald A. Dike and David H. Zucker. Chicago: U of Chicago P, 1970.

Semansky, Chris. <u>Discourse, Institution, and Profession: A Profile of Creative and Critical Practices</u>. Diss. State University of New York at Stony Brook, 1992. Ann Arbor: UMI, 1999.

Shapiro, Alan. "Horace and the Reformation of Creative Writing." <u>American Poetry Review</u> Mar.– Apr. 1992: 7–13.

Shapiro, Karl. <u>The Poetry Wreck: Selected Essays</u> 1950-1970. New York: Random House, 1975.

- - -. "What is not Poetry?" 1960. <u>The Poet's Work: 29 Masters of Twentieth Century Poetry on the Origins and Practice of Their Art</u>. Ed. Reginal Gibbons. Boston: Houghton Mifflin Co., 1979.

Shelley, Percy Bysshe. "A Defence of Poetry." 1840. <u>Shelley's Poetry and Prose</u>. Ed. Donald H. Reiman and Sharon B. Powers. New York: W.W. Norton and Company, 1977. 478–508.

Shelnutt, Eve. "Notes from a Cell: Creative Writing Programs in

Isolation." <u>Creative Writing in America</u>. Ed. Joseph M. Moxley. Urbana, Illinois: National Council of Teachers of English, 1989. 3–24.

Shetley, Vernon. <u>After the Death of Poetry: Poet and Audience in Contemporary America</u>. Durham: Duke UP, 1993.

Sidney, Sir Phillip. <u>A Defence of Poetry</u>. Oxford: Oxford UP, 1966.

Simpson, Louis. "The Character of the Poet." <u>What is a Poet? Essays from the Eleventh Alabama Symposium on English and American Literature</u>. Ed. Hank Lazer. Tuscaloosa: U of Alabama P, 1987. 13–30.

- - - . "Two Responses to 'The Working Line.'" <u>A Field Guide to Contemporary Poetry</u>. Ed. Stuart Friebert and David Young. New York: Longman, 1989. 67–69.

Smith, Dave. <u>Local Assays: On Contemporary American Poetry</u>. Urbana, IL: U of Illinois P, 1985.

Solotaroff, Ted. <u>A Few Good Voices in My Head</u>. New York: Harper and Row, Publishers, 1987.

Spender, Stephen. <u>The Making of a Poem</u>. 1955. Westport, CT: Greenwood Press, 1973.

Stern, Gerald. "What is This Poet?" <u>What is a Poet? Essays from the Eleventh Alabama Symposium on English and American Literature</u>. Ed. Hank Lazer. Tuscaloosa: U of Alabama P, 1987.

Stevens, Wallace. "The Irrational Element in Poetry." 1937. <u>The Poet's Work: 29 Masters of Twentieth Century Poetry on the Origins and Practice of Their Art</u>. Ed. Reginal Gibbons. Boston: Houghton Mifflin Co., 1979. 45–58.

- - -. <u>The Necessary Angel: Essays on Reality and the Imagination</u>. New York: Vintage Books, 1951.

Stone, Robert. <u>Dog Soldiers</u>. New York: Houghton Mifflin Company, 1973.

"Sublime." <u>Oxford English Dictionary</u>. 2nd ed. 1989.

"Sublimation." The Bloomsbury Guide to English Literature. 1990.

Terrell, Carroll F. A Companion to the Cantos of Ezra Pound. 2 vols. Berkeley: U of California P, 1980.

Tolstoy, Leo. What is Art? (1898) Trans. Richard Pevear and Larissa Volokhonsky. London: Penguin Books, 1995.

Treem, Douglas. Personal Interview. 4 November 1999.

Valéry, Paul. The Art of Poetry. Trans. Denise Folliot. Vol. 7 of The Collected Works of Paul Valéry. Bollingen Series XLV. Ed. Jackson Mathews. Princeton: Princeton UP, 1989.

Walzer, Kevin. The Ghost of Tradition: Expansive Poetry and Postmodernism. Ashland Oregon: Story Line Press, 1998.

Warren, Robert Penn. Democracy and Poetry. Cambridge, MA: Harvard UP, 1975.

Weil, Simone. Gravity and Grace (La Pesanteur et la grâce). 1947. Trans. Authur Wills. 1952. Lincoln: U of Nebraska P, 1997.

Williams, C. K. Poetry and Consciousness. Poets on Poetry Series. Ed. Donald Hall. Ann Arbor: The U of Michigan P, 1998.

Williamson, Alan. Eloquence and Mere Life: Essays on the Art of Poetry. Poets on Poetry Series. Ed. Donald Hall. Ann Arbor: University of Michigan Press, 1994.

- - -. Introspection and Contemporary Poetry. Cambridge: Harvard UP, 1984.

Wilson, Edmund. "Is Verse a Dying Technique?" 1934. The Triple Thinkers. New York: Harcourt, Brace and Company, 1938.

Wordsworth, William. "Preface to the Second Edition of Several of the Foregoing Poems, Published with an Additional Volume, Under the Title of 'Lyrical Ballads.'" 1798. The Poetical Works of Wordsworth. Ed. Thomas Hutchinson. London: Oxford UP, 1928. 934–953.

Wright, Charles. Quarter Notes: Improvisations and Interviews. Poets on Poetry Series. Ed. Donald Hall. Ann Arbor: The University of Michigan Press, 1995.

Breinigsville, PA USA
30 September 2010
246442BV00001B/5/P